LEAVING CERTIFICATE

LATER MODERN IRISH HISTORY TOPIC 5

Politics and Society in Northern Ireland 1949–1993

M.E. COLLINS

THE EDUCATIONAL COMPANY

First published 2008
The Educational Company of Ireland
Ballymount Road
Walkinstown
Dublin 12

A member of the Smurfit Kappa Group plc.

© M.E. Collins 2008

0 1 2 3 4 5 6 7 8 9

Editor: Kennedy Print Management Ltd.
Artist: Design Image
Photographs: Getty Images, Alamy, Corbis, British Cartoon Archive, Imagefile, Mary Evans
Picture Library, Photocall Ireland, Ulster Museum Picture Library, Mirrorpix, CAIN, Institute
for Conflict Research, Ronan McCrae
Design and Layout: Design Image
Cover Design: Design Image
Origination: Impress Digital
Printed by:

The Publishers have made every effort to trace and correctly acknowledge copyright holders. If,
however, they have inadvertently overlooked any, they will be pleased to make the necessary
arrangements at the first opportunity.

Acknowledgements

The publisher would like to thank Dr Martin Melaugh, CAIN; Neil Jarman, Institute for Conflict
Research; Jack Pakenham for kind permission to reproduce *The Raft of the Medusa (Ulster
Version)*; Emer McGarry, The Model Arts and Niland Gallery; Rita Duffy for kind permission to
reproduce 'Segregation'; Michelle Ashmore, Ulster Museum Picture Library; Jane Newton,
British Cartoon Archive; The following cartoons are reproduced by kind permission of the
British Cartoon Archive, University of Kent: George Gale, artist, published in the Daily
Telegraph date unknown,   William Papas, artist, published in the Guardian on the 26th
February 1969, Stanley Franklin, artist, published in the Daily Mirror on the 2nd September
1969, John Jensen, artist, published in the Sunday Telegraph on 17th August 1969, David
Myers, artist, published in the Evening News on the 26th February 1969, Wally Fawkes [Trog],
artist, published in the Observer on the 23rd April 1972, Raymond Jackson [Jak], artist,
published in the Evening Standard on the 24th March 1971, Stanley Franklin, artist, published
in the Daily Mirror on the 14th October 1969, Leslie Gibbard, artist, published in the Guardian
on the 29th May 1974, Nicholas Garland, artist, published in the Daily Telegraph on the 11th
July 1972, Leslie Gibbard, artist, published in the Guardian on the 24th May 1974, Stan
McMurtry [Mac], artist, published in the Daily Mail on 29th May 1974.
Cover image: *The Raft of the Medusa (Ulster Version)* by Jack Pakenham

FOREWORD

This book has been designed to meet the requirements for Topic 5 in the Later Modern Ireland section of the new Leaving Certificate History syllabus — Politics And Society In Northern Ireland, 1949-1993.

As the syllabus requires, the Topic is approached from a number of perspectives – politics and administration, society and economy, culture and religion. These perspectives are explored in chapters and the listed 'case studies' – The Apprentice Boys of Derry, The Coleraine University Controversy and The Sunningdale Agreement – are dealt with in detail within the wider perspective to which they belong. Similarly the achievements of the key personalities are also discussed in the context of the events and movements within which they made their contributions.

For ease of study, all chapters are divided into sections, each of which is followed by short questions. These are intended to help students extract the central points from each section and to get them to write short paragraphs which form the building blocks of more extended essays. Exam-type questions for Ordinary and Higher Level Leaving Certificate students are given in a separate chapter at the end of the book.

The use of sources and the development of the skills needed to locate, understand, evaluate and contextualise them are central to the new syllabus. Students can practise these skills on the sources, written and visual, which accompany the case studies. The questions accompanying them are carefully designed to help students understand, evaluate and contextualise the sources. Questions like these form a key part in the new Leaving Certificate history examination. More advice on sources and how to use them is available on the Edco website: www.edco.ie

The new history syllabus aims to help students develop the skills of the historian. But these skills – of research, note-taking, reading for meaning, critical analysis and report writing – are skills which are useful for many walks of life, not just for the study of history. It is hoped that this book will make the acquisition of these skills an enjoyable and rewarding experience.

M.E. Collins
April 2008

Personalities

Introductions to several historical figures are given in purple boxes (key personalities) and green boxes (other personalities) throughout the chapters, with more details about their life and contributions in the text. Biographies of key personalities are also available at the end of the book (see page 118).

CONTENTS

WEBSITES

RTÉ

http://www.rte.ie/

BBC

http://www.bbc.co.uk/history

Channel 4

http://www.channel4.com/history/

National Museum of Ireland

http://www.museum.ie

National Library of Ireland

http://www.nli.ie

National Archives of Ireland

http://www.nationalarchives.ie

CAIN, Conflict Archive on the Internet

http://cain.ulst.ac.uk/

Edco

http://www.edco.ie

Scoilnet

http://www.scoilnet.ie/his/

WEBSITES FOR KEY PERSONALITIES

Terence O'Neill

http://stormontpapers.ahds.ac.uk/stormontpapers/context.html?memberId=4

Conn and Patricia McCluskey

http://cain.ulst.ac.uk/events/crights/pdfs/csj85.pdf

Bernadette Devlin

http://womenshistory.about.com/od/socialism/p/devlin_bio.htm

Ian Paisley

http://www.biographyonline.net/politicians/uk/ian-paisley.html

Brian Faulkner

http://cain.ulst.ac.uk/othelem/people/biography/fpeople.htm

John Hume

http://www.biography.com/search/article.do?id=9346860

http://www.niassembly.gov.uk/members/biogs/jhume.htm

James Molyneux

http://www.ark.ac.uk/elections/fnd95.htm

Margaret Thatcher

http://www.margaretthatcher.org/

Gerry Adams

http://www.sinnfein.org/documents/gerry.html

Seamus Heaney

http://nobelprize.org/nobel_prizes/literature/laureates/1995/heaney-bio.html

THE YEARS OF STABILITY: NORTHERN IRELAND TO 1963

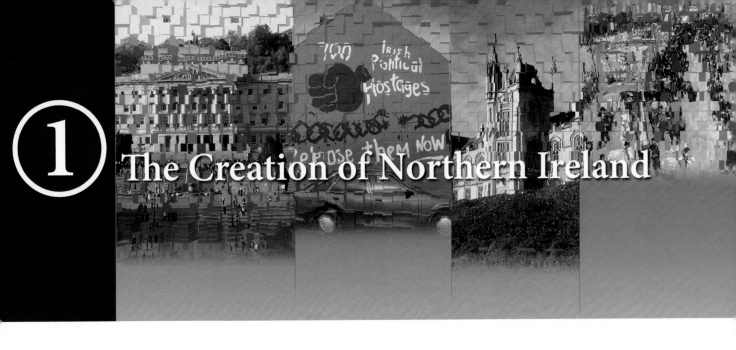

① The Creation of Northern Ireland

IRELAND IN THE UNITED KINGDOM

From 1800 to 1920 the whole island of Ireland was part of the United Kingdom of Great Britain and Ireland. Irish men elected 105 MPs to the United Kingdom parliament in Westminster (London) where they joined with 550 English, Scottish and Welsh MPs to pass laws, decide on taxes and elect a government for the whole of the UK.

Irish people were divided about whether the Union with Britain was good for the country.

- Those who opposed it were called **nationalists**.
- Those who supported it were called **unionists**.
- The division between nationalists and unionists was mainly along religious lines.

NATIONALISTS

- Most nationalists were Catholics who made up 75 per cent of the island's population.
- They felt Irish rather than British and thought that Irish people, not British, should run the country.
- Most of them thought that the Irish economy had suffered under the Union and that the UK government had not treated Catholics fairly.

UNIONISTS

- Most Protestants were unionists. They were 25 per cent of the population but were a local majority in the north east of the island (see map on page 2).
- They felt that they were British as well as Irish because many of their ancestors had come to live in Ireland from Britain during the 17th century plantations. They feared they would lose their British identity if Ireland left the United Kingdom.
- Since Protestants were a minority of the island's population they also feared that a Catholic-dominated Irish parliament would pass laws that would discriminate against them in education, jobs and religious practice.

A Unionist propaganda post card. It shows a Unionist distrust of British promises which remained throughout the 20th century

- North east Ulster, where most Protestants lived, prospered in the 19th century while the economy in other parts of Ireland declined. Protestants feared they might lose that prosperity if Ireland was separated from Britain.

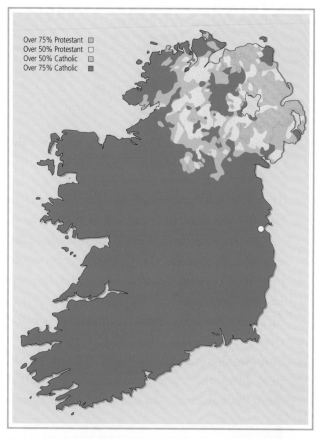

Over 75% Protestant ☐
Over 50% Protestant ☐
Over 50% Catholic ☐
Over 75% Catholic ■

This map is based on the census taken in 1911. In an official document like a census it was not possible to ask people what their political views were but they could be asked about their religion. And since almost all Protestants were unionists and almost all Catholics were nationalists, the religious census also reflected the political divide across the island

CIVIL WAR OR PARTITION

To please the nationalists the British government brought in a **Home Rule Bill** in 1912. It proposed giving Ireland its own parliament and government which would have power over 'home' affairs like transport and education. But the bill left control over most taxes, trade and foreign policy with the Westminster parliament.

The Home Rule Bill was due to become law in 1914. Unionists, led by Sir Edward Carson, opposed it fiercely. They set up a private army, the **Ulster Volunteer Force** (**UVF**) and threatened to resist any Irish government that was set up. Nationalists responded by setting up the **Irish Volunteers** to defend Home Rule.

By 1914 a civil war between unionists and nationalists seemed likely. To avert it, British leaders proposed that Ireland would be **partitioned** (divided) into two parts, a unionist area in Ulster and a nationalist area taking in the rest of the island. Talks about partition were under way when World War I broke out in Europe in August 1914. Both unionist and nationalist Volunteers joined the British army to resist German aggression and the crisis in Ireland was postponed.

But when the war ended in 1918 the situation among nationalists had changed completely. At Easter 1916 some of the Irish Volunteers staged a rebellion in Dublin. They wanted complete independence for Ireland (a republic) rather than the very limited Home Rule offered in the 1912 Bill.

After the British executed the ring-leaders, nationalists began to vote for a political party connected to the 1916 rebels, **Sinn Féin**. In the general election of 1918, Sinn Féin won 73 of the Irish seats but Sinn Féin MPs refused to go to Westminster. Instead they set up **Dáil Éireann** in Dublin and declared that Ireland was a republic. The Irish Volunteers, now calling themselves the **Irish Republican Army** (**IRA**), also began to attack the police and the British army to force them to leave Ireland.

THE GOVERNMENT OF IRELAND ACT (1920) PARTITIONS IRELAND

These developments made Ulster unionists more determined than ever to remain part of the United Kingdom. Carson negotiated with the British Prime Minister, David Lloyd George who brought in the **Government of Ireland Act** in 1920. It divided the island into two parts:
- **Southern Ireland** with 26 counties. In it, Catholics made up about 93 per cent of the population.

and
- **Northern Ireland** with 6 counties. In it about 66 per cent of the population were Protestants and 33 per cent were Catholic.

The Government of Ireland Act in 1920 partitioned Ireland into two states, Southern Ireland (green) and Northern Ireland (orange)

Nationalists rejected Lloyd George's Act. Their war continued until 1921 when they made the **Anglo-Irish Treaty** with him. It replaced 'Southern Ireland' with the **Irish Free State** and promised a Boundary Commission to redraw the border between the Irish Free State and Northern Ireland.

THE CONSTITUTION OF NORTHERN IRELAND

Unionists, on the other hand, welcomed the Government of Ireland Act and quickly began to set up the new state of Northern Ireland. The Act contained its constitution.

- It made Northern Ireland a self-governing region of the United Kingdom, though Article 75 said that supreme power still remained with the Westminster parliament.
- Northern Ireland had its own parliament with a **House of Commons** and a **Senate**. This parliament was to "make laws for the peace, order and good government" of Northern Ireland. It controlled health, education, industry, transport and agriculture and had a very limited power to raise taxes.
- The Northern Ireland Commons had 52 MPs. Lloyd George decided that they should be

Stormont: In 1931 the Unionists built a magnificent parliament building at Stormont Castle. After that the Northern Ireland parliament and government were often called 'Stormont'

elected by **proportional representation** (PR) to ensure that the Catholic minority got its fair share of seats. In 1929, however, the Unionist government replaced PR with the less fair 'first past the post' electoral system. This made it more difficult for nationalists and other parties like Labour to get MPs elected.

- The Commons elected a Prime Minister and a Cabinet which contained ministers responsible for Finance, Home Affairs, Education, etc. The first Prime Minister was **Sir James Craig** (later **Lord Craigavon**) who remained in office until he died in 1940.
- The Westminster parliament kept power over the crown (King/Queen), the armed forces, trade, currency, war and peace. Only it could change the Northern Ireland constitution. It also decided on most of the taxes raised in Northern Ireland and handed the money to the Northern government to spend.
- Because of this voters in Northern Ireland elected 12 MPs to represent them at Westminster.

NATIONALIST RESISTANCE

Lloyd George set up Northern Ireland to protect the Protestant minority within Ireland but in doing so he was unjust to the Catholics left within the new Northern state. Overall they made up about a third of the population but in parts of the west and south they had a local majority (see

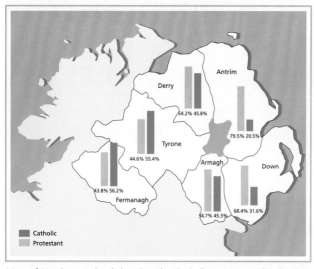

Map of Northern Ireland showing the Catholic/Protestant distribution.

Majority/minority in Northern Ireland: 820,000 Protestants; 430,000 Catholics

map). They were not asked which part of Ireland they wanted to belong to but were assigned to Northern Ireland against their will. The result was that from the start, Northern Ireland had a large minority of dissatisfied Catholic nationalists.

At first nationalists resisted the establishment of Northern Ireland.

- In 1920 there were elections for local councils and nationalists won control of Fermanagh, Tyrone, south Down, south Armagh, Derry city and other councils. They then transferred the allegiance of these councils to the Dáil government in Dublin. To stop this happening again the Unionist government in 1922 changed the method of voting for local councils from PR to 'first past the post' and re-organised the constituency boundaries to ensure that unionists would control most of these councils in the future.
- The IRA attacked the British army and the newly established Northern Ireland police force, the **Royal Ulster Constabulary** (**RUC**). This led to violent sectarian riots in Belfast in 1921 and 1922 when unionist mobs attacked nationalist areas. Over 10,000 Catholics were driven from their jobs and 23,000 were made homeless. Over 300 people died.

THE UNIONIST RESPONSE

The Unionist government took a number of measures to counter nationalist resistance.

- They created '**Special Constables**' to assist the RUC. The 'Specials' were an exclusively Protestant force of heavily armed part-time policemen. They patrolled the areas in which they lived. Their local knowledge helped to defeat the IRA, especially in border areas, though their often-undisciplined behaviour earned the hatred of Catholics. At first there were 'A', 'B' and 'C' Specials and they were intended to be temporary. But while the 'A' and 'C' Specials were soon disbanded, the Unionist government kept the **B Specials** in place until 1970.
- In 1922 the Northern Ireland parliament passed the **Civil Authorities (Special Powers) Act** which gave the Northern government

almost dictatorial powers including the right to intern (imprison) suspected IRA men without trial. The Special Powers Act was intended to be temporary, so parliament had to renew it each year. But in 1933 it was made permanent. It was used almost exclusively against nationalists.

A SULLEN ACQUIESCENCE

The violence of these years hit Catholics hard. Although only making up one third of the population, they suffered two thirds of the casualties. The RUC were mainly Protestant and the Specials were exclusively so, while the Special Powers Act was used to intern Catholics, not Protestants. All this convinced northern Catholics that the new state was hostile to them.

Up to 1925 nationalists hoped that the Boundary Commission, set up under the Anglo-Irish Treaty would redraw the border and restore many of them to the South. But the Commission changed nothing and after that nationalists settled down to a sullen passive resistance to the Northern state.

NATIONALIST DIVISIONS

Almost all nationalists rejected partition and wanted a united Ireland but after 1925 they were divided about how they should behave towards the Northern state.

MODERATE NATIONALISTS: THE NATIONALIST PARTY

Most nationalists were moderates who reluctantly accepted that partition had happened and were prepared to work within Northern Ireland. This view was more common in Belfast and the east of Northern Ireland where Protestants were in a clear majority than in the west.

Moderate nationalists were represented by the **Nationalist Party**. After 1925 it put up candidates for the Stormont parliament and usually won some seats. But Nationalist MPs soon found that the Unionist government did not listen to them

when they raised issues on behalf of their voters. And unlike the opposition party in a normal democracy they could never hope to form an alternative government. That meant that attendance at Stormont was futile and Nationalist MPs often just stayed away.

EXTREME NATIONALISTS: REPUBLICANS

A minority of nationalists were Republicans. They refused to recognise the right of Northern Ireland to exist or to play any part in its institutions. They were most numerous in the west and south where Catholics were often in a majority.

Republicans campaigned constantly for an end to partition and looked to politicians in the South, especially in Fianna Fáil for support. Only a small number joined the IRA and used violence to win a united Ireland but most republicans would have sympathised with the IRA's aims and methods. In theory, the **Sinn Féin Party** represented the republican point of view but they seldom engaged in political activity. When they did and were elected, they followed a policy of **abstention**. That is, their MPs refused to take their seats in Stormont, the Dáil or Westminster. As a result the party had little impact until the 1970s.

UNIONIST ATTITUDES TO NATIONALISTS

Unionists bitterly resented the Catholics' attitude to their state and their demand for the end of partition. They felt that because Catholics refused to recognise the legally established Northern government, they could not trust them to be loyal citizens of the northern state. For that reason, they excluded them from positions of power within Northern Ireland.

THE ULSTER UNIONIST PARTY (UUP)

From 1921 the Ulster Unionist Party (UUP) usually won between 35 and 40 of the 52 seats in the Commons and always formed the government of Northern Ireland. At first it drew support from

Protestants of all classes, who feared a Catholic/nationalist government. But when peace returned and the economy declined in the 1920s some working-class Protestants began to vote for Labour candidates. Craig feared this would split unionism and to stop it he changed the method of electing MPs to Stormont from PR to 'first past the post'.

THE FAILURE OF THE LABOUR MOVEMENT

Craig brought in this change to undermine support for the labour movement. It might have been expected to do well in Belfast because it could appeal to industrial workers, both Protestant and Catholic. But the issue of partition split the labour vote.

- Catholic workers wanted a labour party that backed a united Ireland;
- Protestant workers wanted one that support Northern Ireland's Union with Britain.

This made it difficult for a strong united labour movement to emerge.

Even so, as economic conditions got worse in the mid 1920s the PR system allowed the **Northern Ireland Labour Party** (NILP) which accepted partition, to win some seats as workers on both sides gave it their second preference votes. The change to 'first past the post' voting ended that.

From then on every election became a straight fight between unionist and nationalist, Protestant and Catholic. Protestant workers were warned that if they voted for Labour they were splitting the unionist vote and endangering Northern Ireland. This kept **sectarian differences** at the core of northern politics and made it almost impossible for alternative parties to emerge or alternative policies to be discussed.

GERRYMANDERING LOCAL GOVERNMENT

Unionists also sought to maintain their supremacy by discriminating against Catholics. This was especially noticeable in local government.

- After Sinn Féin won control of many local councils in 1920, the Unionist government changed the method of electing them from PR to the 'first past the post' system in 1922. This made it easier for a united Unionist Party to win seats against the more divided nationalists. As a result 12 councils, including Co. Tyrone, Co. Fermanagh and Derry city which nationalists won in 1920 went under Unionist control.

> **Local government:** Elected county and town councils which took care of sewage, roads, housing, hospitals, etc.

- To ensure that this continued, local Unionists, helped by the Belfast government, carefully drew the boundaries of local council constituencies (called wards) so that a majority of Unionist councillors would be elected even where there were more Catholics than Protestants in the area. This is called '**gerrymandering**'.
- The clearest example of gerrymandering was in Derry City. By 1961 over 60 per cent of its people were Catholic, yet its council had a Unionist majority. This was achieved by dividing the city into 3 wards.
  - The **North Ward** and the **Waterside Ward** in which 7,500 Protestants lived elected 6 councillors each.
  - The **South Ward**, in which 10,000 Catholics lived, elected 8 councillors.

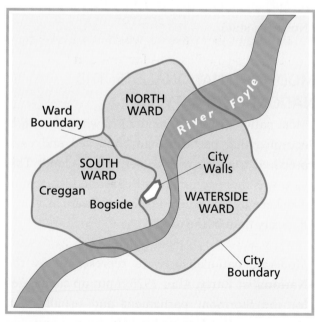

Map showing the electoral divisions (wards) in Derry in the 1960s. Far more people lived in the South (Catholic) Ward than in the other two

Elections and gerrymandering

In Northern Ireland there were elections to three different bodies, Westminster, Stormont and local councils. It is important to know about them and remember which election is being referred to.

- All men and women over 21 could vote for the 12 MPs who sat in the **Westminster parliament**. The elections were by 'first past the post' as they were in the rest of the United Kingdom and there was no gerrymandering.
- Everyone over 21 could also vote for the 52 MPs who sat in the **Stormont parliament**, again using the 'first past the post method' from 1929. Most constituency boundaries were fairly drawn but because Northern Ireland had a Protestant majority of 66 per cent, the Unionist Party always won between 35 and 40 of those seats.
- Seventy three **local councils** were elected using the 'first past the post' method from 1922. In most councils there was a clear Catholic or Protestant majority, so no gerrymandering was necessary. Only in the west of Northern Ireland where numbers were fairly evenly balanced did gerrymandering occur.

- This arrangement left the Unionist Party in control of Derry Corporation from 1922 until the end of the 1960s. As we shall see later, this had major implications for jobs and housing.

THE PROPERTY QUALIFICATION

In elections to both the Westminster and Stormont parliaments all men and women over 21 could vote for MPs. But this was not true in elections for local councils. There the right to vote depended on a **property qualification**. It meant that:

- Only a householder and his/her spouse could vote in local elections.
- A business man had a vote for each building he owned, up to a maximum of six.
- Adult children living at home and lodgers in rented accommodation did not have a vote.

In the 1920s there was a property qualification for local council elections in Britain and the Irish Free State as well as Northern Ireland. It existed because local councils could raise a tax on property (the rates) and it seemed fairer that only those who paid that tax should be able to vote.

But the property qualification prevented many poor people, Protestants as well as Catholics, from voting for the councils which affected so many aspects of their lives. As democratic ideas grew, it was replaced by one person/one vote in the South in the 1930s and Britain in the 1940s. But the Unionist government refused to change and the property qualification stayed in place in Northern Ireland into the 1960s.

DISCRIMINATION IN JOBS

Because the Unionist Party controlled central and local government they were able to decide who got jobs and they saw to it that Catholics were kept out of all but the most poorly paid posts (see page 42 for more detail).

- Although in theory, Catholics were supposed to make up a third of the RUC, in practice they never reached more than 10 per cent and there were no Catholics among the higher ranks.
- In 1920 when the Unionist government took over, there were Catholics at the top of the civil service but they were not replaced when they retired. Only a small number of Catholics joined the civil service after that and they did not reach the higher ranks in either central or local government.

Unionists explained their discrimination in several ways

- *Catholics did not apply to join the civil service or the police.* This was largely true. Catholic schools did not encourage young people to apply for civil service jobs and the few Catholics who did reported that their neighbours regarded them as having sold out. But it may also have been that Catholics did not apply because they knew they would not be welcomed or gain promotion.
- *Catholics lacked the education to get the top jobs.* It was true that Catholics as a whole were

poorer and less well educated than Protestants up to the 1950s but there were individual Catholics who were university graduates and they were not given senior positions as, for example, judges.

THE UNIONIST SIEGE MENTALITY

Unionist discrimination against Catholics arose from fear and insecurity. They were always aware that, while they were 66 per cent of the population of Northern Ireland, they were only 25 per cent of the population of the whole island. A number of factors added to their sense of being besieged.

- Although Protestants were a majority within Northern Ireland, they feared that one day northern Catholics would outnumber them and vote the six counties back into a united Ireland. This fear arose from the fact that Catholics tended to have more children than Protestants. From the 1920s to the 1960s around 40 per cent of school children were Catholic, even though Catholics were only 33 per cent of the population as a whole. By preventing Catholics getting jobs, unionists hoped to encourage them to emigrate and so remove that danger.

- In the South, nationalist leaders constantly talked about ending partition and reuniting Ireland. Articles 2 and 3 of De Valera's 1937 Constitution claimed to rule the whole island of Ireland. In practice southern politicians did nothing about it but that was no comfort to nervous unionists.

- Unionists' security depended on British support but unionists did not really trust the British. They set Northern Ireland up in 1920; if it suited them, they could hand it over to the South any time they wished. That this fear was well founded became clear in 1940 when Winston Churchill offered Irish unity to Eamon de Valera in return for Irish support in World War II. Churchill did not bother to consult the Northern Ireland leaders about his offer.

UNIONISTS MORE SECURE AFTER WORLD WAR II

Éamonn de Valera turned the offer down and the unionist position strengthened after that. British political leaders were angered by the South's neutrality and they appreciated the support of the Unionist government during the war. Northern Ireland farmers helped to supply Britain with food; Northern Ireland industry produced uniforms, parachutes, ships and planes for the war effort. Above all Northern Ireland provided the military and naval bases from which the Royal Navy and RAF (and later the Americans) could patrol the North Atlantic searching for German submarines and protecting the convoys which carried vital supplies to Britain from the United States. When the war ended in 1945 the unionists were more secure within the United Kingdom than they had ever been before.

QUESTIONS

1 Who were the nationalists and what did they want? Describe the distribution of nationalists in Ireland in 1920.

2 Who were the unionists and what did they want? Describe the distribution of unionists in Ireland in 1920.

3 When was the Government of Ireland Act passed and what did it do?

4 Describe (a) the parliament and (b) the government of Northern Ireland. What was Northern Ireland's relationship with Britain?

5 How did northern nationalists resist the establishment of Northern Ireland?

Describe two ways in which the Unionist government dealt with their resistance.

6 Name the main nationalist parties within Northern Ireland and say what the policy of each of them was.

7 Give two reasons why the Labour Party found it difficult to win seats in Northern Ireland.

8 Unionists were in a clear majority in Northern Ireland yet they continued to feel insecure. Explain why that was and describe three things they did to ensure that they remained in power.

② Culture and Society in Northern Ireland: The Marching Tradition

CULTURE IN A DIVIDED SOCIETY

Partition created a divided society in Northern Ireland in which each community kept to itself.

- The Catholics/nationalists saw themselves as Irish and rejected the northern state. They kept their cultural ties with the rest of the island and developed these within their schools, newspapers and clubs.
- The Protestants/unionists considered themselves British and looked to London for cultural inspiration and leadership.

NATIONALIST CULTURAL ACTIVITIES

In the Stormont years the Catholic minority retreated into its ghetto. Catholics met and worked with Protestants as individuals but the communities had little to do with one another.

Nationalists self-consciously preserved and cultivated their own cultural identity. Catholic schools played a large part in this. They taught students the Irish language and Irish history which were not part of the official school curriculum. Boys' schools usually played hurling or Gaelic football, rather than rugby or soccer. The **Gaelic Athletic Association** (GAA) was the most public expression of identity that the nationalist community had. It was unaffected by partition, with the six northern counties remaining part of the all-Ireland circuit of matches. Inside the North, many Catholic parishes had a GAA club, which was often the centre of social activity.

Some nationalists also belonged to the **Ancient Order of Hibernians**, (AOH) a Catholic equivalent to the Orange Order, though it was not as significant among Catholics as the Orange Order was among Protestants. It had links with the Nationalist Party and organised parades on St Patrick's Day and on 15 August. But these parades were small and the Unionist government restricted them to areas where Catholics were in a majority. The RUC did not allow nationalists to parade in town centres and the 1954 Flags and Emblems act made it possible for the police to remove the republican tricolour or the papal flag if a unionist objected. After the fall of Stormont republicans began holding parades to commemorate the Easter rising, Bloody Sunday and the hunger strikes.

THE LACK OF A CULTURAL TRADITION

Cultural identity was a more difficult issue for unionists than for nationalists. Before partition, some of them had followed developments in the South where Protestants like Douglas Hyde, W B Yeats and Lady Gregory had been leaders of the cultural revival of the early 20th century. But most unionists rejected the cultural revival because it seemed to lead to Irish nationalism. They thought of themselves as British and looked to Britain (by which in practice they meant England) as the source of their cultural identity.

For the Unionist government, that removed any need to encourage a distinctly Northern Irish culture in literature or the arts after 1921. The official school curriculum required students to study English literature and English history, with very little reference to Ireland. There was no support for local artists or writers, nor any attempt to develop a distinctive 'Ulster' cultural identity. In 1951 the Stormont government failed to name an artist to represent Northern Ireland at the Festival of Britain because, according to the Minister for Education, Northern Ireland was as much a part of Britain as Yorkshire.

THE LOYAL ORDERS

The only feature of Northern Ireland culture that got official unionist recognition was the tradition of parading by the **Loyal Orders**. That was the collective name given to the Orange Order, which was by far the biggest, the Apprentice Boys of Derry, the Royal Black Institution and a number of smaller organisations. For at least a century before partition, these organisations had held parades that commemorated significant events in the history of Protestants in Ireland. Since the events commemorated were usually Protestant victories over Catholics, the aim of the parades was to give Protestants a sense of common identity and unite them in their determination to resist any threat from the Catholic/nationalist majority within the island.

THE ORANGE ORDER

The Orange Order was by far the biggest and most important of the loyal orders. It was founded in 1795 after a riot between Catholics and Protestants in Co. Armagh. After Home Rule became a possibility in the 1880s, leading unionists cultivated it as a weapon in their struggle against nationalism. The Order became intimately involved in the Unionist Party. It was represented on the party's governing body, the **Ulster Unionist Council** and it was almost impossible for an Ulster Unionist politician to succeed unless he was an Orangeman. From 1922 to 1969 all but three ministers in the government of Northern Ireland belonged to the Order.

Courtesy: Corbis

An Orange march in Belfast. Note how the street has been cleared of traffic

The Orange Order is organised into lodges, most of them based in towns or villages. To join the Order, a member has to be invited by the local lodge. All members are committed to '... *diligently study the Holy Scriptures ... love, uphold and defend the Protestant religion*'. They will also '*strenuously oppose the fatal errors and doctrines of the Church of Rome, and scrupulously avoid countenancing (by his presence or otherwise) any act or ceremony of Popish worship*' and '*by all lawful means, resist the ascendancy of that Church*'. But they also should abstain '*from all uncharitable words, actions, or sentiments, towards* [their] *Roman Catholic brethren*'.

The Order has a democratic structure. Local lodges elect representatives to District Lodges. They in turn elect representatives to the County Grand Lodge which then elects the **Grand Lodge of Ireland**. It is headed by the **Grand Master of the Orange Order**. But although the Grand Lodge and the Grand Master were the public face of Orangeism, they have little control over the activities of local or District Lodges.

By the 1960s there were about 1400 Orange lodges in Ulster with over 100,000 members. Almost every village in Northern Ireland had its Orange hall where the local lodge met. The hall was also the centre of social activity for the Protestant community, providing space for dances, games, band practices and meetings.

Orangemen gathering for a march

Courtesy: Imagefile

On the surface the Orange Order looked like a religious organisation but in fact it was almost completely political. Its main purpose was to hold parades celebrating historic events that were important to the unionist community such as the victory of the Protestant King William of Orange over the Catholic King James at the Battle of the Boyne (1690) or the Battle of the Somme in World War I in which so many men from Ulster died. For most Orangemen parading to commemorate these events is the main purpose of their membership.

THE TWELFTH

While many local lodges held small parades at different times throughout the summer marching season, the biggest day in the Orange calendar was the **Twelfth** (of July) which commemorated the battle of the Boyne. Usually there were a number of large parades on that day – a big one in Belfast and others in some agreed location which rotated among the districts. Tens of thousands of Orangemen and women and their families took part in these parades.

For unionists the Twelfth was a great family day out. Each local lodge saw to catering and transport for its members and arranged for a band to lead them. In the morning local lodges marched in their own areas, often to a church service. Even those members who seldom went to church turned up to parade with their lodge. Then the members and their families went by bus to one of the bigger marches.

At the big parade solemn men in bowler hats and Orange collarettes marched behind colourful banners showing King Billy (William of Orange) on his white horse or other Protestant heroes or scenes from the bible. Uniformed bands accompanied the marchers. The main instruments were pipes, accordions or flutes and some bands had huge Lambeg drums on which large men beat out the rhythm. They played traditional airs like '*The Sash my father wore*' or '*The Green Grassy Slopes of the Boyne*', and other songs which were more explicitly anti-Catholic. From the 1960s 'blood and thunder' or 'kick the pope' bands emerged. Often from working class areas of Belfast or from Scotland, they were more openly sectarian than the more traditional bands. Some of them had links to Protestant paramilitary organisations like the UVF.

After the march, families picnicked while listening to speeches from unionist leaders or Protestant churchmen. They extolled the virtues of Protestantism, praised its defence of civil and religious liberty and reasserted its defiance of the papists or Catholics. The whole day evoked and celebrated a common Protestant past and a Protestant identity in the face of the threat of universal Catholicism.

ORANGE MARCHES AND THE NATIONALIST COMMUNITY

Many Orange marches passed through predominantly Protestant districts and went off peacefully. But some created tension when they went near or through Catholic areas. Under Stormont, the RUC protected these marches on the grounds that they were 'traditional' and Catholics could do nothing about them.

Unionists in the 1990s often claimed that up to 1969 Catholics watched the parades with interest and sometimes even took part. That was not how Catholics remembered them. They were offended by the triumphal anti-Catholicism of the songs and the speeches and resented the fact that Orangemen could parade through nationalist areas while their own parades were restricted. These resentments, combined with the offensiveness of some of the songs and the drunkenness of some of the marchers, inevitably led to disturbances on many Twelfths even before 1969.

The Sash My Father Wore
For those brave men who crossed the Boyne have not fought or died in vain
Our Unity, Religion, Laws, and Freedom to maintain,
If the call should come we'll follow the drum, and cross that river once more
That tomorrow's Ulsterman may wear the sash my father wore!

Chorus:
It is old but it is beautiful, and its colours they are fine
It was worn at Derry, Aughrim, Enniskillen and the Boyne.
My father wore it as a youth in bygone days of yore,
And on the Twelfth I love to wear the sash my father wore.

The first verse and chorus of a favourite Orange song. The old man opposite is wearing a typical orange sash

The Crest of the Apprentice Boys of Derry. List the symbols on it and explain them

THE APPRENTICE BOYS OF DERRY (CASE STUDY)

Much smaller than the Orange Order but just as central to unionist identity is the organisation known as **the Apprentice Boys of Derry**. Its main purpose is to commemorate the **Siege of Derry** of 1688-89 which took place during the war between the Protestant King William of Orange and his Catholic father-in-law, King James II. The story of Derry's heroic siege is an important part of the unionists' mythology and self-image.

DERRY'S HEROIC SIEGE

In 1688 when the war began, Protestants from across Ulster took refuge in the walled city of Derry. James's army commander ordered them to let his troops in. While the city's leaders debated what to do **13 apprentice boys**, shouting *'no surrender'*, locked the gates against the Catholic forces on **7 December**.

The banner of the Browning Club, one of the eight 'parent clubs' of the Apprentice Boys. Browning was one of the heroes of the siege

In April King James himself arrived and called on the city to surrender to him. The Governor, **Colonel Lundy**, suggested giving up but the inhabitants still insisted on *'no surrender'*. Lundy fled from Derry and among Protestants his name became another word for 'traitor'.

James's army surrounded the city and a long siege began. They stopped food getting to the city's inhabitants who began to starve. To survive people had to eat dogs and rats. About 4,000 died of hunger and disease. Finally after 105 days, the Williamites sent three ships into the Foyle. On **28 July 1689** one of them, the ***Mountjoy***, broke through a barrier the enemy had placed across the harbour and ended the siege.

REMEMBERING THE SIEGE OF DERRY

From the early 1700s Protestants held parades to commemorate the siege but they became bigger and more elaborate from the 1880s, as the threat from Catholics/nationalists grew. They were staged by the **Apprentice Boys of Derry**, an organisation based in the city.

It consists of 8 'Parent Clubs' which are based in the magnificent **Memorial Hall**. Six of the clubs are named after leaders of the siege; the other two are the Apprentice Boys Club and the No Surrender Club. Each Parent Club has branch clubs scattered around Northern Ireland, the republic, England, Scotland and Canada. Altogether there are about 200 branch clubs and the total membership of the Apprentice Boys is about 12,000. Membership *'is open to anyone who professes Christ through the reformed Protestant faith'* and only men may join.

The Apprentice Boys are led by their General Committee. It is based in Derry and is dominated by the Parent Clubs. It organises two main events each year. Early in December it commemorates the closing of Derry's gates by the apprentices and on 12 August the arrival of the *Mountjoy*. Other, smaller parades can be held at other times and branch clubs can organise local parades for themselves.

The main celebration is on 12 August, making that an important date in the North's marching season. At its height during the Stormont era, up to 40,000

An Apprentice Boys' collaret (sash) in the organisation's crimson

people came from Ulster and abroad to watch. In 1964, for example, it was reported that the parade was two and a half miles long with more than 100 clubs and 100 bands taking part. It took 70 minutes for them to pass Carlisle Square.

The Apprentice Boys, dressed in their crimson collarettes, assembled on the Mall Wall, which overlooked the Catholic ghetto of the Bogside. Symbolically this represented the supremacy of Protestants over Catholics within the city. Then, accompanied by their bands, they marched around the walls of Derry and attended a service in the Church of Ireland Cathedral, St Columb's. The ceremonies included laying a wreath at the war memorial in memory of Ulster people who died in the two world wars and initiating new members. That ceremony can only take place in Derry. At the smaller parade in December an image of 'Lundy' is symbolically burnt on a bonfire.

THE APPRENTICE BOYS AND THE ORANGE ORDER

There was no formal link between the Apprentice Boys and the Orange Order but many men belonged to both organisations. The Apprentice Boys were more religious and less political, though

One of the gates in Derry's walls. It is Ireland's only remaining walled city and one of the few in Europe

in the Stormont years they too had seats in the Ulster Unionist Council. They withdrew from it in the 1970s. While it was never as important for a politician to belong to the Apprentice Boys as to the Orange Order, many Unionist leaders, including Lord Brookeborough, Terence O'Neill and Brian Faulkner were members. Ian Paisley remained a member even after he left the Orange Order in 1965.

Ian Paisley left the Orange Order in the 1960s to set up his own Independent Orange Order, but he remained faithful to the Apprentice Boys

THE SYMBOLIC IMPORTANCE OF THE SIEGE

From the start the story of the siege of Derry became for Protestant Ulstermen a symbol of the heroic defence of their freedom against Catholic rule. Always aware that in Ireland as a whole, Catholics outnumbered them by three to one, they saw themselves as constantly under siege, just as their ancestors had been in 1688–89. And like those heroic ancestors, they too must be brave, defiant ('*no surrender*') and constantly on the alert against traitors (*Lundys*) who might sell them out.

This self-image remained and even grew after Ireland was partitioned. Unionists still saw themselves as a besieged minority within Ireland. The Union with Britain and the state of Northern Ireland protected them from Catholic domination, just as the walls of Derry had protected their ancestors in the 17th century. This point was made year after year in the speeches that accompanied the parades, like this one from 1958:

'The border is a secure bulwark to [the Ulsterman's] religious faith and his political freedom under the ample folds of the Union Jack, as the old grey walls of Derry were nearly three centuries ago.'

But by the time Northern Ireland was set up, Derry had become a predominantly Catholic city. In local elections in 1920 nationalists won a majority of seats on the Corporation and Craig feared that the Boundary Commission might give it to the South.

Even though that did not happen, unionists still could not accept the possibility that Derry might pass under nationalist control. That would have been a symbolic reversal of what happened in 1689 and therefore a betrayal of the unionist community. To prevent that happening, the

This mural from the 1980s, echoing Derry's siege story, shows how important that story still is for Northern Protestants

Unionist government consistently gerrymandered local elections in Derry (see page 6). This generated Catholic resentment and contributed significantly to the start of the civil rights movement in the 1960s.

THE APPRENTICE BOYS AND THE 'TROUBLES'

It was no accident that the outbreak of violence in 1969 was connected to Apprentice Boys marches in Derry.

- In October 1968 when civil rights demonstrators planned to march inside the city walls, the Apprentice Boys called a special parade. This gave the strongly unionist Home Affairs minister, William Craig an excuse to ban both marches (see page 47) and violence followed.
- The 12 August parade in 1969 sparked off the 'battle of the Bogside' and the introduction of British troops (see page 51).

For most of the 1970s and 1980s Apprentice Boys parades were banned completely or confined to the mainly Protestant Waterside district. But as community relations in Derry improved at the end of the 1980s, the nationalist dominated council agreed to let the parade resume within the city and in 1989, at the third centenary of the siege, it organised a pageant to celebrate it.

QUESTIONS

1 What were the main features of Catholic cultural identity in Northern Ireland and how were they protected?

2 How was Protestant cultural identity different from that of Catholics?

3 What were the Loyal Orders?

4 Write a short essay on the Orange Order and its marching tradition.

5 What was the origin and purpose of the Apprentice Boys of Derry?

6 How are the Apprentice Boys organised?

7 Describe the main Apprentice Boys parades.

8 Why was the story of the siege of Derry so important to unionists' sense of identity?

DOCUMENTS: A, B AND C

1: The Marching Tradition

A: It is in its way a great folk festival bringing people from all over the north, from Liverpool and Canada and from across the border in Donegal. And it has a good humour which is not so marked in other celebrations of Ulstermen. There are no slogans except for those recollecting the relief of the city in 1689, no speeches and no resolutions. Just a three hour parade through the narrow streets and along the walls.... They wear a traditional uniform of bowler hats and crimson sashes... On either side of the flags, men march with drawn swords... In the morning a large crowd attended a service in the cathedral to hear a sermon counselling restraint towards people of different religious persuasion with steadfastness in defence of the Protestant heritage (from: Fergus Pyle, *'Apprentice Boys are cheerful in the rain'*, *Irish Times*, 14 August 1967).

> Try to include words or phrases from the documents in your answers.

B: The Siege of Londonderry, when the Catholic Irish came within an ace of over-running the Protestants, began in December 1688. In three centuries it has never lost its potency (power) and immediacy as a symbol for unionists for they believe that the enemy is forever at the gate, waiting for the sentry to fall asleep. The siege has been commemorated … not so much as a pleasant piece of folklore but as an event of continuing political significance... [It] serves as an icon to demonstrate the immutable (unchanging) nature of the conflict. The Protestants draw from it the moral that Britain can only be trusted up to a point, that Lundys must be guarded against and that endurance and resolution are in the end the only way to hold the fort. The siege, in the minds of many men, is still going on... (from: David McKittrick, *Dispatches from Belfast*, Belfast, 1990, p. 29)

C: To most of those who march, the marching period is a celebration of their history, culture and religion while to most of those who do not, it is at best a colourful spectacle, at worst an expression of sectarian triumphalism (Michael Hall, *Exploring the Marching Issue: Views from Nationalist North Belfast*, *Island Pamphlets*, 64, 2004, p. 1)

QUESTIONS ON THE DOCUMENTS

Comprehension

1 Give three of the elements of the 'great folk festival' described in Document A. How did he think it was 'different from other celebrations of Ulstermen'?

2 What, according to the author of Document B, does the Siege of Londonderry still symbolise for unionists?

3 What, according to Document C, is the difference between 'those who march' and those 'who do not'?

Comparison

4 Which of the views of marching in Document C is expressed by the authors of Document A and by the author of Document B? Support your answer by referring to the documents.

Criticism

5 Which of the Documents, A or B, would be most helpful to a historian studying the Apprentice Boys of Derry?

DOCUMENTS: D AND E

2: Marching and violence

In August 1969 it seemed likely that the Apprentice Boys annual parade in Derry would spark off a violent reaction and desperate attempts were made to persuade them to cancel it.

D: As the days passed, the mood in Derry grew tenser... Having demolished minority rule, Derry nationalists were not prepared to permit a massive Orange demonstration of triumphant tribalism through a predominantly Catholic city...

> Try to include words or phrases from the documents in your answers.

But the Apprentice Boys were unyielding. They were going through with their celebrations. They insisted on the right of unionists to march in any part of Northern Ireland at any time. If there was trouble it would not be their responsibility. It would be the duty of the authorities to deal with it. All the urgings of Hume and others that in the circumstances there was no chance of the parade passing off peacefully were rejected. The government might hope that the Apprentice Boys would draw back from the brink but ... it was not prepared to make history by banning their remembrance of the Relief of Derry. The occasion was sacred to Orangemen and unique in the unionist tradition... (from: Frank Curran, *Derry: Countdown to Disaster*, Dublin, 1986, pp 128–30).

E: On the eve of the march in August 1969 I asked an Orangeman of my acquaintance, the kindest and most decent of men, why it was necessary to keep up these obviously provocative celebrations. He looked at me in mild surprise and then said grimly: 'We have to show them who's master – that's why' (from: Patrick Macrory, *The Siege of Derry*, London, 1980, p. 355).

QUESTIONS ON THE DOCUMENTS

Comprehension

1 What did people in Derry try to persuade the Apprentice Boys to do in August 1969 and what was their response?

2 Why, in the opinion of the author of Document D, did the Unionist government fail to stop them from marching?

Comparison

3 What light does the Orangeman's answer, quoted in Document E throw on the attitude of the Apprentice Boys described in Document D?

Criticism

4 Do you think the author of Document D is fair to the Apprentice Boys? Support your answer by quoting from the document.

Contextualisation

5 Using information contained in these five documents discuss the significance of the Apprentice Boys of Derry and their parades to the cultural identity of northern unionists.

③ Culture and Society in Northern Ireland: Poetry and the Arts

ULSTER POETS

Not all Ulster Protestants were content that their cultural identity should be expressed only through the marching of the Loyal Orders. Although they got no official encouragement from the Unionist government, there were individual voices who expressed a need for a different kind of cultural engagement.

Northern Ireland produced several fine poets in the years after 1920. The most famous of them was **Louis MacNeice** (1907-1963). He spent most of his adult life in Britain where he was one of a group of influential writers. He worked for the BBC and used his position to promote the work of other Ulster writers.

JOHN HEWITT (1907–85)

A poet who stayed in Belfast was **John Hewitt**. He worked for many years in the Belfast Museum and Art Gallery. A socialist who supported the Union while rejecting unionism, Hewitt was involved in most of the literary movements of his time. He understood the division within Ulster, writing of himself:

> Mine is the historic Ulster, battlefield
> Of Gael and planter,
> Certified and sealed
> By blood…

After World War II he urged Ulster artists to develop a 'regional identity' writing that '*Ulster,*

considered as a region and not as a symbol of any particular creed, can, I believe, command the allegiance of every one of its inhabitants'. Apart from his poetry, his main contribution to this project was to collect and publish ballads sung by the weavers who made Ulster prosperous in the 18th and 19th centuries.

Although Hewitt spent ten years in England from 1957, other new talents emerged in the 1950s. One was **Sam Thompson**. A Protestant labour activist working in Harland and Wolfe, he lost his job for opposing sectarianism. He used this experience in his most successful play, *Over the Bridge*. It offended Unionist leaders with its treatment of bigotry in the Belfast shipyards.

A NEW GENERATION OF POETS

In the early 1960s a new generation of poets emerged. Including both Catholics and Protestants, many of them came from poor families yet managed to get a good education thanks to the welfare state. Several of them met and became friends in the non-sectarian surroundings of Queen's University in Belfast.

SEAMUS HEANEY

Seamus Heaney was typical of this generation of northern poets. Born in 1939, he is the eldest of nine children on a fifty-acre farm called Mossbawn in Co. Derry. A scholarship allowed him to attend St. Columb's, a Catholic boarding school in Derry. At

Seamus Heaney (1939–) Heaney's poems first came to public attention in the mid 1960's when he was active as part of a group of poets who were recognised as a 'northern school' within Irish writing.

eighteen he went to Queen's University where he studied Irish and Latin. Later he trained as a teacher. In the early '60s he became involved in a writers' group started by an English lecturer, Philip Hobsbaum, where young poets such as Heaney, Michael Longley, Derek Mahon and James Simmons could meet to read and discuss their work.

His first collection of poems, *Death of a Naturalist*, was widely praised after it appeared in 1966. Other poets from the group also published their work and critics began to talk of a school of 'Northern poets'. As well as Heaney, they included Derek Mahon, Michael Longley, Paul Muldoon, Medbh McGuckian and Ciaran Carson.

But apart from being roughly the same age, all they shared was the fate of being born into a society deeply divided along religious and political lines. While many of them had supported the civil rights movement when it began they were not prepared for the violence which broke out in 1969 and reacted differently to it.

The troubles darkened the mood of Heaney's work in the 1970s, as he became preoccupied with the issue of poetry's responsibilities in such circumstances.

He wrote: *the problems of poetry moved from being simply a matter of achieving the satisfactory verbal icon to being a search for images and symbols adequate to our predicament'* (from *'Feeling into Words' Preoccupations*, 1980). For all the Northern poets the problem lay in whether to respond to each atrocity and be accused of exploiting suffering or to ignore it and be accused of indifference.

In most cases Heaney chose to approach the northern violence indirectly. His poems appear on the surface preoccupied with the countryside of his childhood (*At the Potato Digging*), with ancient bog-bodies (*Tolland Man*) and ancient Irish literature (*Sweeney Astray*) but echoes of current violence break through in stray lines and references. Other poets accused him of indifference to the suffering, especially after he went to live in the South in 1971.

FIELD DAY

In 1980 Heaney was one of a group of artists who set up **The Field Day Theatre Company** in Derry. They included the poet Tom Paulin, the actor Stephen Rea and the playwright Brian Friel.

The first play produced by Field Day was Friel's *Translations*. It dealt with the British plan to map Ireland in the 1830s. With its themes of cultural misunderstandings and the power of the conqueror to take over even the place names of the conquered, it cast an oblique light on the issues in the northern conflict. Field Day went on to produce a series of pamphlets on cultural issues. The aim behind these was to create a cultural debate which might in time lead to a better understanding among the North's divided people.

NEW CULTURAL DEVELOPMENTS

Around Europe in the 1960s governments began to invest more in arts and culture and this happened in Northern Ireland too.

- An **Arts Council** was set up in 1962. It supported many forms of artistic activity including music and painting was well as literature.
- Money was also spent on raising the standard of the **Ulster Museum** and helping it to build

up a collection of modern Irish pictures and sculptures as well as of artefacts connected to Ulster history.

- One of the most important developments was the creation of the **Ulster Folk Museum** at Cultra in Co. Down in 1964. It collects and displays houses and tools from Ulster's past and studies and preserves folk traditions. It made no distinction between Protestant and Catholic but drew equally from both communities in keeping with Hewitt's idea of a regional identity shared by both 'planter' and 'Gael'.

- A similar idea lay behind the expansion of the **Public Record Office of Northern Ireland** which stored the state's historical archives and of the **Linen Hall Library**, a private institution dating back to the 18th century. Since 1969 it has put together a unique collection of posters, handbills, cartoons and other relics of the troubles which would otherwise have been thrown away.

NORTHERN PAINTERS AND THE TROUBLES

In the visual arts there were similar developments. Like the poets, artists were the beneficiaries of the improved education system and greater state funding of the arts from the 1960s. In the 1970s and 1980s a number of artists emerged who attempted to represent the impact of the troubles in visual images.

One of the most important of them was Jack Pakenham, who wrote in 1994,

> *To have ignored the Troubles, to have said, as many Art purists did, that human suffering and tragedy have no place in visual art would have been, in my opinion, reprehensible. If art is merely about titillating the eye and the nervous system, then it is neglecting that which it does best, namely touching the deepest emotions of which man is capable* (Jack Pakenham, 'Ceasefire 1994' Circa 1995, pp. 21–22).

Artists like Pakenham and Rita Duffy produced dark brooding pictures in which the pain, both physical and psychological, that the violence inflicted on individuals, is expressed in powerful and moving images.

*Pakenham's **The Raft of the Medusa (Ulster Version)** is based on a classical image of survivors of a ship wreck. Note how many figures wear masks and gaze away from each other, emphasising the sense of lonely despair*

CULTIVATING CULTURAL DIVERSITY

From the 1980s both the British and Irish governments recognised that these cultural activities could help to create bridges between the communities around which peace might grow. Various conferences and summer schools,

*Rita Duffy's **Segregation** hints at the unseen forces that keep ordinary people from meeting. While the men dispute, long bony hands come from nowhere to separate women and children*

including one named in honour of John Hewitt, received generous funding and allowed people from all communities to try to understand the things that united and separated them within their divided community.

EDUCATION FOR MUTUAL UNDERSTANDING

Many believed that the separate education of Catholic and Protestant children was one reason for conflict between the two communities. To counter this, the British government in 1989 added **Education for Mutual Understanding** to the school curriculum. Its was:

> ' ...about self-respect, and respect for others, and the improvement of relationships between people of differing cultural traditions.'
> (Northern Ireland Curriculum Council, 1990)

A significant part of the programme was to encourage pupils from Catholic and Protestant schools to meet and engage in joint activities so as to remove the sense of separation between the communities which lay behind a good deal of the conflict.

QUESTIONS

1 Write a short essay on the life and work of Seamus Heaney.

2 How did the cultural scene change in Northern Ireland from the 1960s?

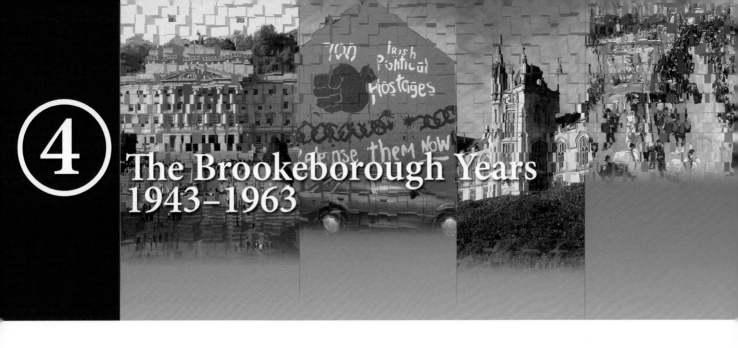

④ The Brookeborough Years 1943–1963

SIR BASIL BROOKE (LORD BROOKEBOROUGH) 1888–1973

In 1943 in the middle of World War II, Sir Basil Brooke (who was later given the title of **Lord Brookeborough**) became Northern Ireland's third Prime Minister.

A landlord from Co. Fermanagh, Brookeborough had earned a reputation for efficiency in his previous post as Minister for Agriculture. But he was a divisive figure. Catholics saw him as deeply sectarian. He had been responsible for reviving the **Ulster Volunteer Force** in 1920 and had helped to establish the hated **B Specials**. At an Orange parade in 1933 he said:

> 'Many in this audience employ Catholics, but I have not one about my place. Catholics are out to destroy Ulster...If we in Ulster allow Roman Catholics to work on our farms we are traitors to Ulster...I would appeal to loyalists, therefore, wherever possible, to employ good Protestant lads and lassies...'

When he took over, Brookeborough spoke of the need for unity in the war effort but he made no gesture towards the Catholic minority. He explained:

> 'I knew I could not invite the Nationalists to run in double harness with the Unionists. At the time they were entirely non-co-operative especially in regard to any effort during the war.' (Robert Fisk, *In Time of War*, Gill & Macmillan Ltd, Dublin, 1983, p. 457)

In fact Brookeborough had little reason to fear the nationalists. By 1945 the Unionists were in a far stronger position than they had been before.

- Many British politicians resented the South's neutrality in the war and were grateful for the part the North had played in defeating Nazi Germany.

- In the Cold War, which began in 1946, they continued to appreciate the strategic importance of Northern Ireland, out on the edge of the Atlantic, and were unlikely to urge it to re-unite with the neutral South.

Courtesy: Getty

The Northern Irish Prime Minister Lord Brookeborough standing before a Unionist election poster in 1949. What message is the poster sending?

WESTMINSTER'S ATTITUDE TO NORTHERN IRELAND

Westminster politicians were also reluctant to get involved in Northern Ireland. Since 1920 a convention had grown up among them that they must not discuss the internal affairs of Northern Ireland. They argued that these were none of their business because the Government of Ireland act made Stormont responsible for how Northern Ireland was run. This convention made it impossible for concerned British MPs to get the Westminster parliament to discuss Unionists' treatment of Catholics.

THE LABOUR GOVERNMENT AND THE UNIONISTS

When the war ended there was a general election in Britain. The Labour Party, led by Clement Atlee won a landslide victory. At first Unionists were dismayed because traditionally the Labour Party was more sympathetic to nationalists than the Conservatives. A few of them even talked of leaving the United Kingdom and becoming a independent Dominion like Canada.

But they need not have worried. Although some Labour MPs did form a pro-nationalist group, the Friends of Ireland, Atlee and his ministers had no intention of interfering in Northern Ireland or of doing anything that might encourage a united Ireland.

THE GROWTH OF THE LABOUR MOVEMENT

In fact Brookeborough's biggest concern at that time was the success of Labour candidates in the 1945 Stormont election. Although the Ulster Unionist Party won 34 seats out of 52, Labour candidates gained 7 seats in Belfast, several from the Unionists. This was partly due to the general growth of socialism in post-war Europe, and partly due to dissatisfaction among voters with the rationing and housing shortages that continued after the war.

THE SOUTH DECLARES A REPUBLIC

In 1949 a Coalition government in Dublin decided to leave the British Commonwealth and become a republic. Brookeborough saw his opportunity to defeat labour. He called an election, proclaiming:

Our country is in danger... we fight to defend

our very existence and the heritage of our Ulster children... Our determination to remain under the Union Jack should be immediately and overwhelmingly reaffirmed (D. Harkness, *Northern Ireland*, p. 20).

He urged all unionists to show their support for the Union by voting for the Unionist Party. They did and the Labour MPs lost their seats.

The South's decision strengthened the unionists in other ways. Atlee's response to it was the Ireland Act. This recognised the independence of the republic but it also promised that:

'...in no event will Northern Ireland or any part thereof cease to be part of his Majesty's dominions and of the United Kingdom without the consent of the Parliament of Northern Ireland.' (David McCullagh, *A Makeshift Majority*, Dublin, 1998, p. 106)

This was the firmest guarantee that the unionists had ever received from Britain and secured their position within the United Kingdom.

LABOUR INTRODUCES THE WELFARE STATE

Between 1945 and 1951, the British Labour government introduced major reforms in health, education and social welfare along the lines proposed in the 1942 **Beveredge Report**. These reforms were extended, step by step, to Northern Ireland.

But the North could not afford to pay for them out of its own limited tax income, so Brookeborough made an agreement with the London government that Britain would subsidise them. In return, taxation in Northern Ireland would be kept at the same level as in Britain, and the Northern budget would be submitted to the British Treasury for approval.

> **The principle of parity:** The idea, dating from the 1920s that, because Northern Ireland was part of the United Kingdom, its taxes and social services should be on a **par** (i.e. equal) with those in England, Scotland and Wales.

This took control of much of the taxation and spending away from the Northern government but Brookeborough quickly realised that the result was worthwhile. The British subsidy gave northern citizens far better health care, social service and education than they could have afforded to pay for themselves. And these services were also much better than the South could afford to provide for its citizens.

REFORMS IN HEALTH

A number of Health Acts replaced the old health system and created the **National Health Service** (NHS).

- It guaranteed free medical care to all patients.
- A Hospitals' Authority took over the supervision of hospitals.
- Local health authorities took charge of general health care, child and maternity services, sanitation and home help schemes.
- The Northern Ireland General Health Services Board was set up to supervise these services.
- Tuberculosis, as bad a scourge in the North as in the South, was tackled by the NI Tuberculosis Authority.

THE PROBLEM OF THE MATER HOSPITAL

As always the sectarian issue caused problems. The Mater Hospital in Belfast was owned by the Mercy nuns. They feared that the Hospitals' Authority might threaten their independence but the Health Minister insisted that the Mater be either fully in or fully out of the scheme. The nuns refused to join which meant that the Mater got no building grants or state payments for its patients.

As a result, Catholics found themselves having to support their hospital by voluntary subscriptions, while paying through their taxes for the public health system. This caused considerable resentment until a compromise was finally worked out in 1972.

REFORMS IN EDUCATION

An Education Bill in 1947 set up a new system of primary, secondary and third level education.

- Primary schooling was to end at twelve. The year before that, pupils took an examination called the 'Eleven Plus'.
- The 25 per cent of pupils who passed the examination got free places in grammar schools and could go on to university, for which there were generous scholarships.
- The 75 per cent of pupils who failed went to secondary modern schools. They got a non-academic education and most of them left at fourteen or fifteen.
- State schools, under the control of local councils, got full grants for building and maintenance and their pupils did not have to pay fees. Catholics would not send their children to these schools which as a result were almost exclusively Protestant.
- Catholic-owned schools, which refused to join the state system, had their building grants raised from 50 per cent to 65 per cent in spite of protests from some unionists. Up to 80 per cent of their pupils got scholarships but the rest had to pay fees.

THE IMPACT OF EDUCATIONAL REFORMS

These reforms came into effect in 1948. Though the Catholic community resented the lower grants, they gained a lot from them. The new system opened the chance of secondary and university education for bright boys and girls whose families were to poor to give them the opportunity without state aid. This produced a new generation of well educated and articulate young Catholics in the 1960s. They resented the discrimination they experienced under Unionist rule and they led the struggle to reform it.

REFORMS IN SOCIAL WELFARE

A comprehensive system of National Insurance was introduced in 1948.

- Insurance contributions were collected from all employed people and generous pensions or cash payments were made to the old, the sick, the unemployed and the widowed.
- As Unionist politicians regularly pointed out throughout the 1950s, this raised the amount paid in old age pensions, children's allowance and unemployment assistance well above the level that existed in the South in the 1950s (see table A, p. 27).

Council housing estate

REFORMS IN HOUSING

Northern Ireland had a major problem with housing, made worse by the Germans bombing of Belfast during the war. A survey in 1943 estimated that 200,000 new houses had to be built to clear the slums and provide decent homes for all citizens. In 1945 the **Housing Act** provided for the building of subsidised houses which would be rented to poor tenants. Some were to be built by local councils but the Act also created the **Northern Ireland Housing Trust** with powers to clear slums and build houses across Northern Ireland.

By 1961 over 95,000 new houses had been built, about 40,000 of them by private builders. The rest were built either by local councils or by the Housing Trust. Most councils and the Housing Trust gave these houses to tenants on the basis of need rather than political allegiance. But in 12 of the 73 local councils this was not the case.

These councils were all **west of the Bann**, and were controlled by Unionists even though the majority of the local population was Catholic. The most notorious of them were Derry, Dungannon

> **'East of the Bann', 'West of the Bann'**
> The river Bann flows into Lough Neagh from the Mourne Mountains and then from the lough into the sea. It thus divides Northern Ireland roughly into east and west, a division which also has political significance. East of the Bann Protestants are in a majority, west and south of it, Catholics dominate.

and Omagh. Since a house carried with it the right to vote in local council elections, councils often left poor Catholic families on waiting lists while they gave houses to less needy Protestants. This created resentments which boiled up into resistance in the mid-1960s (see page 43).

ECONOMIC PROBLEMS AFTER THE WAR

The North's traditional industries were farming, linen and shipbuilding. All had prospered during the war but after it they began to decline. In agriculture many farms were small and uneconomic and unlikely to survive as independent units. In linen many firms were old-fashioned with major structural weakness and it seemed probable that they would close with the loss of many jobs. Shipbuilding held up well into the 1950s but by 1960 faced growing competition from more efficient shipyards in Poland and Japan.

GOVERNMENT ECONOMIC POLICY

These problems meant that unemployment would rise and Brookeborough feared that would increase support for the Northern Ireland Labour Party. The government took steps to create new jobs.

- In 1945 the **Industries Development Act** gave factory sites as well as loans and grants to new industries.
- In the 1950s the Unionists got the approval of the London government to spend more on building new hospitals, schools and university accommodation to bring Northern Ireland infrastructure up to British levels.
- In 1956 the government set up the **Northern Ireland Development Company** to attract overseas firms to replace the vanishing jobs. It had some success in attracting foreign firms. Nationalists complained that most new industries were located east of the Bann but this was probably due more to the desire of the firms to be near to main transport routes and a skilled workforce than to any government policy.

These policies produced some successes.

- Linen production declined sharply after 1950 and the number of workers fell from 56,000 in 1954 to 34,000 ten years later. But the government did succeed in getting multinational clothing firms, especially those working with synthetic fibres, to set up branches in Northern Ireland because of the pool of skilled weavers available there.
- In 1950 Harland and Wolff shipyard employed 21,000 people most of them in skilled, well-paid jobs. These numbers remained constant through the 1950s partly because the Royal Navy bought ships. This changed in the early sixties when the British government policy of rationalising shipbuilding led to a loss of 11,500 jobs between 1961 and 1964. Since almost all workers in the shipyards were Protestants, this alarmed the Unionist Party and was one of the reasons why Brookeborough was forced to retire in 1963.

Between 1950 and 1962 industrial production in Northern Ireland rose by 50 per cent. This, together with the building of new houses, increased the number employed by 10,000. But unemployment stayed between 6 per cent and 10 per cent, twice the average in Britain. Northern Ireland remained the poorest part of the United Kingdom.

TRANSPORT POLICY

The job creation programme was accompanied by an attempt to improve communications. Railways were taken over by the government and the Dublin-Belfast line was run jointly by the two governments. To limit losses about half the tracks were closed by 1970 including one of the two linking Belfast and Derry. The central government also took over responsibility for all trunk roads from the local authorities and improved their standard greatly. In 1962 they opened Ireland's first motorway though Derry people noted it only went to Dungannon.

AGRICULTURAL

Agriculture was the North's most important industry which in 1950 still employed 14 per cent of the workforce. Britain was the main customer for Northern Ireland farm produce and the British government subsidised the prices farmers got. This kept farm incomes relatively high and encouraged the development of intensive farming of pigs and poultry. Subsidies gave northern farmers the money to mechanise their farms. By 1960 there were 70,000 tractors (compared with less than 1000 in 1939). This reduced the need for labour and increased productivity by 80 per cent.

BROOKEBOROUGH AND THE NATIONALISTS

Many members of the Unionist Party were hostile to these policies. They resented having to pay higher taxes and disliked the increased welfare payments to poorer citizens, especially nationalists. They also objected to the government's increased involvement in the economy which they regarded as 'socialist' if not actually 'communist'.

Brookeborough rejected these doubts. He believed that better social welfare benefits might convince the Catholic minority to accept Northern Ireland. In elections throughout the 1950s Unionists used figures like those in table A to point up the advantage of being part of the United Kingdom.

Up to the mid-1950s Brookeborough had been more conciliatory towards Catholics than many of his colleagues wanted.

Table A

Comparison of social welfare benefits in the North and South		
Benefit	North	South
Children's allowance for each child after the first	5 shillings a week	2 shillings a week
Unemployment pay for a single man	24 shillings a week	15 shillings a week
Unemployment pay for a married couple	40 shillings a week	22 shillings a week

A Unionist view of the relationships between North and South in the 1950s. The 'poor Eire-worker' however was much more likely to head for Britain than Northern Ireland

- He supported increasing the grant to Catholic schools even when this was fiercely opposed by some unionists, including the young Ian Paisley.
- He supported the easing of the **Special Powers Act** and encouraged the RUC to ban Orange parades in nationalist areas.

But he did nothing that might undermine unionist supremacy.

- When the British government brought in one person, one vote in local government elections in Britain, he insisted on keeping the property qualification for voting in Northern Ireland.
- After unionists protests that Southerners were moving North to find work, he brought in work permits and made them work for three years before being entitled to social welfare. No such limits were placed on Irish people working in Britain.
- After riots during the coronation of Queen Elizabeth II in 1953, he backed the **Flags and Emblems Act** of 1954 against the advice of the police. This Act allowed the RUC to remove any flags other than the Union Jack and became an endless source of conflict between the nationalists and the police.

THE ANTI-PARTITION LEAGUE

After the war, nationalists, north and south, continued to demand an end to partition. The Nationalist Party won ten seats in the 1945 election and their MPs entered Stormont for the

first time since the 1930s. The election of a Labour government in Britain briefly raised their hopes but these were dashed when Atlee's Ireland Act guaranteed Northern Ireland's place in the United Kingdom. They set up the **Anti-Partition League** and with the help of the republic's foreign minister, Seán McBride, a former leader of the IRA, began a campaign to bring the issue to the attention of the world. The world was not interested.

*Seán MacBride, the leader of **Clann na Poblachta**, during the 1948 election. He was foreign minister in the coalition that followed and a tireless campaigner against partition*

THE IRA'S BORDER CAMPAIGN

These developments led to a revival of the IRA which had declined after the war. It attracted young nationalists frustrated by the lack of progress towards a united Ireland. Between 1951 and 1955, the IRA raided a number of military barracks, looking for arms. The most successful raid was on Gough Barracks in Armagh in June 1954.

In December 1956 the IRA announced a campaign against 'British imperialism' in Northern Ireland and called on the whole population of the North to help them. This declaration reflected IRA ignorance of the reality of Northern Ireland where the majority of the community cherished their Union with Britain.

The campaign was fairly intensive in the first half of 1957. It consisted mainly of attacks on border posts and police barracks. Two policemen and several IRA members were killed and in the South Sinn Féin won two seats in the general election.

Brookeborough used the **Special Powers Act** to intern IRA suspects without trial. In the South, Fianna Fáil won the general election in March 1957 and de Valera brought in internment too. After that the campaign faded away and the IRA finally called it off in 1962, bitterly noting:

> 'foremost among the factors responsible for the ending of the campaign has been the attitude of the general public whose minds have been deliberately distracted from the supreme issue facing the Irish people, the unity and freedom of Ireland.' (D. Harkness, *Northern Ireland Since 1920*, Helicon, Dublin, 1984, p. 131)

The campaign was a complete failure. Confined to isolated districts near the border it hardly touched the lives of most people in the North. After it IRA leaders began to re-examine their tactics. They recognised that violence led nowhere. Some retired; others turned to Marxist revolutionary socialism and began to support campaigns against social and economic grievances like unemployment and housing.

THE LACK OF RECONCILIATION

In the Stormont election of 1959 the Unionist Party did well and there were signs that in a few places Catholics voted for them rather than for Sinn Féin candidates who represented the republican position. Some unionists also noted that the IRA's campaign got almost no support from northern nationalists and began to wonder if northern Catholics were at last becoming reconciled to their separation from the rest of Ireland.

This led a few prominent unionists to suggest that Catholics might be encouraged to join the party and perhaps even stand as Unionist candidates. This modest proposal produced howls of outrage from traditional unionists as well as from the Orange Order and Ian Paisley. Brookeborough hurriedly disowned the suggestion.

This episode and a campaign in the early 1960s among unionist workers in Belfast to ensure that any redundancies in the ship building industries would be confined to Catholics all indicated that even after forty years the majority of unionists would resist any attempt to reach out towards the minority and include them as full citizens within the northern state.

QUESTIONS

1 Write a short paragraph on Lord Brookeborough up to 1945.

2 What was the Ireland Act? Why was it passed and how did it reassure unionists?

3 What is meant by the term 'Welfare State'? Describe the changes it produced in (a) health, (b) education (c) social welfare and (d) housing in Northern Ireland.

4 What economic problems did Northern Ireland face between 1945 and 1963? Describe the steps that Brookeborough's government took to deal with them.

5 Describe Brookeborough's relationship with the nationalist minority.

6 What was the IRA? Describe its border campaign and explain why it failed. List two ways in which that failure affected Northern Ireland.

THE YEARS OF STABILITY: NORTHERN IRELAND TO 1963

THE END OF THE BROOKEBOROUGH GOVERNMENT

By the early 1960s many in the Unionist Party were growing dissatisfied with Brookeborough's government. By then in his seventies, he was still popular with unionist voters but his attitudes were out of tune with the times. His successor, Terence O'Neill wrote of him that:

> ' ...the tragedy of his premiership was that he did not use his tremendous charm and his deep Orange roots to try to persuade his devoted followers to accept some reforms.' (T. O'Neill, *Autobiography of Terence O'Neill*, Hart-Davis, 1972, p. 47)

Most criticism of the Brookeborough government came from middle-class unionists, many of them businessmen. They resented the fact that the Unionist Party had been led by the landed gentry since 1921. Their main concern was with economic policy. Job losses in the main industries of linen, shipbuilding and aircraft manufacture increased in the early 1960s and the government did not seem to be doing enough to protect jobs or create new industries. Workers too were worried. The Northern Ireland Labour Party (NILP) won several Unionist seats in the 1962 Stormont election. Most of these were in Belfast and there was evidence that both Protestant and Catholic workers voted for them. This was a serious concern for the Unionist Party.

LEADERS OF THE UNIONIST PARTY

The two leading ministers in Brookeborough's Cabinet were rivals to succeed him as Prime Minister. They were the Finance Minister, Terence O'Neill and the Minister for Home Affairs, Brian Faulkner.

Captain Terence O'Neill (1914–90): Captain Terence O'Neill came from a land-owning family in Co Antrim but had been educated in England. He served in British army during the war, then returned to Northern Ireland where he was elected to Stormont in 1946.

○ Able and aloof, O'Neill was more at home in a London drawing room than in an Orange hall.

He made little attempt to disguise his contempt for many of his fellow Unionist MPs while his haughty manner and upper class English accent alienated them. In politics he was a moderniser who wanted greater economic planning to meet the rapidly changing conditions of the early 1960s and to encourage inward investment by foreign firms. He felt that economic success would encourage Catholics to overcome their hostility to Northern Ireland and allow it to move away from sectarian politics.

Brian Faulkner (1921–77): Brian Faulkner came from a wealthy family engaged in the linen industry. During the war he worked in his father's factory and was always uncomfortably aware of his lack of military experience.

- Elected to Stormont in 1949, Faulkner was an able and ambitious politician who had a good relationship with ordinary party members. He supported traditional unionism including the right of the Orange Order to march in Catholic areas. In 1959 he was the Minister of Home Affairs responsible for enforcing internment to defeat the IRA campaign. Rural and working class unionists who disliked O'Neill's modernising ideas and policies looked to him for leadership.

TERENCE O'NEILL BECOMES PRIME MINISTER

When Brookeborough resigned suddenly in March 1963, Faulkner was in America and an inner group in the party chose O'Neill as the new Prime Minister without an election. At forty-eight, he was a generation younger than Brookeborough but Unionists resented the lack of an election. His habit of acting alone or with the advice of a small group of advisors also caused resentment. That meant that O'Neill could never rely on the whole-hearted support of Unionist MPs or even of his Cabinet ministers.

A MORE RELAXED ATMOSPHERE

O'Neill took over at a time when the old Protestant/Catholic rivalries were easing around the world.

- Religious divisions grew less acute after the election of Pope John XXIII in 1958. He backed the idea of **ecumenism** (reconciliation between Christians), encouraged Catholics to work with Protestants and called the Vatican Council to reform the Catholic Church.
- In the United States, where a majority of citizens were Protestant, a Catholic, John F. Kennedy was elected President in 1960.

In Ireland too, nationalist/unionist rivalries were also declining.

- In the Republic, Seán Lemass replaced de Valera as Taoiseach in 1959. Lemass made it clear that he was more interested in economic development in the South and co-operation with the North than in an immediate end to partition.
- In the North, many young Catholics and Protestants, especially those with a university education, felt the old antagonisms were out of date and wanted to work together for a common future.

GESTURES OF RECONCILIATION

O'Neill responded to this new atmosphere with a number of gestures towards Catholics.

- He was the first northern Prime Minister to visit a Catholic school.
- When Pope John XXIII died in 1964, he sent official condolences and had flags fly at half mast.

These were small courtesies, which would have passed unnoticed elsewhere, but in Northern Ireland they were almost revolutionary and aroused protests from extreme unionists like Ian Paisley.

THE LEMASS VISIT

O'Neill's most dramatic gesture was his invitation to Sean Lemass to visit Stormont. He was impressed by Lemass's conciliatory references to the North and he recognised the desirability of cross-border co-operation on transport, power, agriculture and tourism. But characteristically he did not consult other ministers about the invitation and this weakened him in the debate which followed.

Lemass's visit on 14 January 1965, was quickly followed by an O'Neill visit to Dublin and meetings between the Ministers of Commerce and Agriculture, and their opposite numbers from the South. The meetings were well received in the Republic and among northern nationalists. Lemass encouraged the Nationalist Party, led by

One of the meetings between O'Neill and Lemass

Eddie McAteer, to become the official opposition in the Stormont parliament, a role they had refused to occupy since 1920. But among some unionists, always fearful of betrayal, they aroused fears and O'Neill came under attack from Paisley and his supporters.

PLANNING FOR ECONOMIC DEVELOPMENT

However, O'Neill's main aim was not reconciliation with the nationalist community but the defeat of the NILP which was attracting the votes of dissatisfied unionist workers. He hoped to do this by encouraging economic growth, especially in the unionist heartlands east of the Bann. In Britain and the republic in the early '60s the idea that governments should plan the future development of the economy was beginning to take hold and he wanted to apply this idea to Northern Ireland and its economic problems.

O'Neill set up a number of committees to report on future economic policy. No Catholic was appointed to any of these committees.

- The **Benson Report** in 1963 recommended improving road transport and the closing of uneconomic railway lines. One of those closed was the line linking Tyrone and Fermanagh with Belfast and Derry.
- The **Matthew Report** in 1964 suggested that the government limit the expansion of Belfast and encourage 'growth centres' elsewhere.
- The **Wilson Report** in 1965 urged the government to encourage foreign firms to set up in Northern Ireland with the aim of creating 65,000 new jobs by 1970. But it warned that it would be difficult to persuade incoming firms to set up west of the Bann because it was too remote and inaccessible and proposed that most development take place in the east.

O'Neill also set up an Economic Council to implement these plans and put the Minister for Commerce, Brian Faulkner, in charge of economic development. Faulkner produced a package of incentives which soon brought in big overseas companies including ICI, Dupont, Grundig, and

Courtaulds. By 1965, unemployment had fallen to its lowest level for ten years and in the Stormont election of that year the NILP lost seats.

DEVELOPING THE EAST, NOT THE WEST?

Most inward investment went to areas east of the Bann and nationalists noted that the main 'growth centres' were also in the east. Derry, as Northern Ireland's second city and with a high level of unemployment, had expected to be one of them but instead the area chosen for development was near the mainly Protestant Lurgan/Portadown area, where a new city was set up. To the annoyance of nationalists it was named Craigavon after Northern Ireland's first Prime Minister.

The government defended the development of the east on the grounds that the west was 'too remote' and that foreign firms did not want to go there. But nationalists did not believe them. They thought that the Unionist government was deliberately developing its Protestant heartland while neglecting the west where Catholics were in a majority. The outcome of the campaign to locate Northern Ireland's second university in Derry strengthened this conviction.

THE COLERAINE UNIVERSITY CONTROVERSY (CASE STUDY)

THE EXPANSION OF UNIVERSITY EDUCATION

The education reforms of the 1940s increased the demand for university places. In Britain in 1961 the government set up the Robbins Committee to look into the matter and in 1964 it recommended the establishment of new universities in areas where there had been none before.

UNIVERSITY EDUCATION IN NORTHERN IRELAND

The same issue arose in Northern Ireland where Queen's University in Belfast was the only university.

It had expanded rapidly through the 1950s and the question arose: should it continue to expand or should another university be set up elsewhere?

At first the government thought that the Robbins Committee might make recommendations for Northern Ireland too but when it did not they set up their own Committee in 1963. It was chaired by an Englishman, Sir John Lockwood who was the head of Birbeck College in London. Three of the remaining seven members were English. One Catholic was invited to serve on it but when he was unable to do so, no other Catholic was appointed. The **Lockwood Committee** was instructed '*to review the facilities for university and higher education in Northern Ireland, having regard to the report of the Robbins Committee and to make recommendations*'.

DERRY AND MAGEE COLLEGE

Many people assumed that any new university would be located in Derry. With a population of 70,000, it was Northern Ireland's second biggest city and already had a third level institution at **Magee College**. Magee was an odd institution which had been set up in the 19th century with a gift from a Mrs Martha Magee to train Presbyterian clergy. When Irish universities were reorganised in 1908 it was left out and had very little money for staff or facilities.

Magee had close ties with Trinity College and they continued even after partition. Students spent two

The main building at Magee. Although looking rather fine, it was very out of date by 1964 and in need of repair

years in Magee then went to Trinity to complete their degrees. In 1953 the Northern Ireland government agreed to provide more funds for Magee but the college was small, poorly funded and its buildings were in poor repair.

When the Lockwood Committee was set up many in Derry expected it to recommend that Northern Ireland's second university should be built around Magee College. A university would also create jobs and give a boost to Derry's depressed local economy.

THE LOCKWOOD COMMITTEE (1963-65)

The Lockwood Committee quickly decided that Queen's could not easily expand and that a new university was desirable. They then had to decide where to locate it. Derry, Coleraine, Armagh and the planned new city of Craigavon all competed for the prize. The Committee quickly ruled out Armagh and Craigavon and the final decision came down to a choice between Derry and Coleraine.

The Committee had a number of requirements.
- Was there a suitable site for the university?
- Was there accommodation for students and staff?
- Was there local support, including finance from the local council?
- Were there local opportunities for research or for co-operation with local industries?

ASSESSING DERRY AND COLERAINE

The members of the Committee met representatives of Derry and Coleraine and visited the areas.
- The Derry delegation offered Magee as the site of a new university but they were so confident of success that they did not discuss alternative sites or where students were to be accommodated.
- The Coleraine representatives had to start from scratch. They referred to new universities being set up in England and offered to provide a site on which to build one. They also pointed out that the nearby holiday resorts of Portstewart and Portrush had plenty of hotels and boarding houses which were empty all winter and so available for staff and students at no cost to the government.

The members of the Lockwood Committee then discussed the two offers.

They were not impressed by Derry's case.
- Magee was too small to house a new university and its buildings were in a poor state.
- New buildings would be necessary but the delegation did not offer a site for them or promise financial support.
- There was no accommodation for staff or students and expensive hostels would have to be built.
- There was very little industrial development in Derry and it seemed unlikely that there would be much in the future.
- The sectarian tensions in Derry made it an unsuitable site for a university.

Coleraine impressed them much more.

One of the buildings of the new University of Coleraine

It had offered a site on which building could begin quickly.
- It could house staff and students quickly and cheaply.
- There had been some industrial development and there could be more in the future.
- It was solidly Protestant and so free of sectarian tensions.

○ Perhaps the fact that it was fairly near Derry would compensate that city for the loss of Magee.

As a result of these deliberations, the Lockwood Committee recommended that Magee be closed and a new university be built in Coleraine.

DERRY'S RESPONSE TO THE LOCKWOOD REPORT

As rumours of this decision spread, anger rose in Derry. In January 1965 a University for Derry Committee (UDC) was set up, chaired by John Hume. Containing both unionists and nationalists, it claimed that *'government policy seems directed towards isolating the north-west in general and Derry in particular'*. It organised an all-party public meeting to protest and later met O'Neill and his Minister of Education to press Derry's case.

The Lockwood report appeared on 10 February. On 18th the UDC called for a two minutes silence. It was widely observed and pubs and shops closed in protest. A 2000 strong motorcade, led by the Unionist mayor and a Nationalist MP headed for Stormont to protest to the government.

O'NEILL AND THE 'NAMELESS, FACELESS MEN'

The next day O'Neill met secretly with some leading Derry Unionists. This meeting later caused controversy and what happened at it is not very clear. It seems they wanted to him to keep Magee open but they did not press for the new university to be located in Derry rather than Coleraine. Their reason for this seems to have been the fear that an influx of staff and students might upset the delicately balanced Unionist control of the council. In a rambling discussion, they expressed similar fears about any industrial development in the city. O'Neill seems to have shared these concerns, because in the minutes of the meeting he is quoted as asking: if Derry industrialised *'how is it possible to insure against a radical increase in R C papes?'* (G. O'Brien, *'Our Magee Problem: Stormont and the second university'* in G. O'Brien (Ed) Derry and Londonderry, Dublin, 1999, p. 645).

In May Dr Robert Nixon, a Derry Unionist MP, claimed that O'Neill had met with 'nameless, faceless men' from Derry who had opposed the creation of a university there. The government response was to deny that any conspiracy existed and to expel Nixon from the party. They also ignored a petition signed by 15,000 people asking for an enquiry.

RC = Roman Catholic
Papes = papists, an offensive term for Catholics

THE FINAL DECISION

Given the attitude of the Derry Unionists and of O'Neill himself, it is not surprising that the Stormont government decided to accept the recommendations of the Lockwood Committee. This decision led to a three-day debate in the Stormont parliament. Unionists from west of the Bann joined with nationalists in protesting at the decision but in the end the Report was accepted by 27 votes to 19. However O'Neill did agree to leave Magee open as a branch of the new university.

The government's decision pleased unionist voters east of the Bann. That was important in O'Neill's campaign to limit support for the NILP which he thought was more important than winning over Catholics. In the Stormont election later that year the Unionist Party did well and support for the NILP declined.

WHY DID THE LOCKWOOD COMMITTEE CHOOSE COLERAINE?

Many in Derry believed that the Unionist government had influenced the recommendation of the Lockwood committee. There is no evidence to support this and Lockwood himself denied it. But they may have been influenced by civil servants who told them that industrialists were reluctant to set up in Derry because it was 'too remote'.

The real problem with the Lockwood Committee was its political naivety. Three of its eight members were English and several of the others had spent most of their lives outside Northern Ireland. They knew little of local political sensitivities. They chose Coleraine on the kind of rational grounds – availability of a site and of student lodging – that the Robbins Committee used in England. But these grounds took no account of the North's political realities.

THE IMPACT OF THE DERRY UNIVERSITY CONTROVERSY

The loss of the university was a huge blow to the people of Derry, unionist as well as nationalist. For a brief moment they had been united in demanding it and they had been denied.

Nationalists tended to blame the decision on the government's anti-Catholic prejudice and saw it as part of a deliberate policy of blocking economic development west of the Bann. John Hume made this point in a speech in July 1965:

> '...the plan stands clear. The minority in Northern Ireland resides mainly in the western counties ... To develop these areas is to develop areas opposed to the government and to lose the few Unionist seats held there. The plan is therefore to develop the strongly unionist Belfast-Coleraine-Portadown triangle and to cause a migration from west to east Ulster, redistributing and scattering the minority so that the Unionist Party will not only maintain but strengthen its position.' (speech in London, 30 July 1965).

This belief undermined any faith nationalists had in O'Neill's good intentions. He might speak fair words to them but his deeds showed him up in his true, unionist, colours. The only hope now of making the unionist establishment listen to Catholic grievances was direct action. This lesson contributed to the emergence of the civil rights movement.

But unionists living west of the Bann were also badly hit by the government's neglect of the area. Central government decisions on the university, on railways, on the location of multinational companies and on the development of growth centres affected them too. They were angry and said so at Unionist Party meetings where they got little sympathy. But deeply entrenched sectarian attitudes made it impossible for them to make common cause with nationalists against the government. Instead when Ian Paisley and others criticised O'Neill, they found sympathetic listeners in the west.

QUESTIONS

1 Why did many people in Northern Ireland think Brookeborough should retire in 1963?

2 Name the two leading politicians who were rivals to lead the Unionist Party after him and write a short paragraph on each of them.

3 Why did Terence O'Neill become Prime Minister in 1963? Why was that a good time to take over the leadership?

4 Outline the gestures that O'Neill made towards the minority community and explain why he made them.

5 How did O'Neill deal with the economic problems facing Northern Ireland in the mid-1960s?

6 Why was the location of Northern Ireland's second university such an important issue? What was the result of the controversy?

DOCUMENTS: A AND B

1: Magee College

Two news items:

A: *'Weakness in the way Derry presented its case'*
Derry's claim is based on the fact that in Magee University College it has the nucleus of a second university and that it would be foolishness to start afresh in some other centre when up to 300 students are now able to complete the major part of their university studies in Magee...

Where Derry lags is in not having a representative 'big names' promotion committee to push its claim and to launch a university foundation fund with a target of several hundred thousand pounds, as in other centres across the water which have got new universities. Derry has left it to a Corporation sub-committee ... and the Corporation has promised a contribution of a three penny rate in the initial ten years of any new university project. Three pence ... in Derry means an annual contribution of about £5000 (*Irish Times,* 2 January, 1965).

> Try to include words or phrases from the documents in your answers.

B: The whole student body from Magee College, Derry are to go in specially chartered buses to Stormont today in support of the resolution calling for the raising of the College to full university status. Placards to be carried will include "Queens £6,500,000 since 1953; Magee £27,000 (*Irish Times,* 13 February 1965).

QUESTIONS ON THE DOCUMENTS

Comprehension

1 Read Document A. Where does it come from? Was it written before or after The Lockwood Report became public?

2 What, according to the writer of Document A, is Derry's claim to a university based on and how was that claim weak?

3 In Document B what were the students from Magee planning to do and what messages were they sending to the public?

Comparison

4 Does the information in B support or contradict the opinion expressed in A about Derry's campaign? Support your answer by referring to the document

Criticism

5 Which of these two documents would be more useful to a historian studying the controversy? Explain your answer by referring to the content of the documents.

DOCUMENTS: C AND D

2: Response to the choice of Coleraine for a University

C: *Extract from a pamphlet:*

...In the past year or two even more determined attempts have been made to weaken and depopulate the western three counties in the following ways:

1. There were two separate railway lines to Londonderry. In the interests of economy it became necessary to close one of them. The one to be 'axed' traversed the western region. This has left Fermanagh, Tyrone and practically all of the county of Londonderry with no railway whatever. The other three counties have two separate systems...

2. In order to further strengthen the relatively prosperous east, the government of Northern Ireland is to build a New City in County Armagh. Mr. Geoffrey Copcutt was engaged as its chief designer. He is an Englishman who came here after planning Cumbernauld New City near Glasgow. After over a year's work he resigned saying, "I have become disenchanted with the Stormont scene." He suggested the abandonment of the New City and that the development of Londonderry should be concentrated upon in order to give the province a reasonable balance.

3. The government in February 1965 accepted the Wilson Plan for economic development. This report outlined four centres for rapid industrial development all within a 30 mile radius of Belfast and none in the western counties.

4. In February, 1965, the government also accepted the Lockwood Report. Here, Londonderry was rejected as the site for a new university, in spite of the fact that Magee University College, a hundred year old institution, is at present providing the first two years of university education in certain subjects. Copcutt in his statement said "Londonderry is the obvious choice to expand as the centre for higher education outside Belfast . . . It could prove the most promising way of unifying the present populations and integrating future immigrant communities." (from: *Londonderry, One Man, No Vote*; Patricia McCluskey and others, *The Campaign for Social Justice*, February, 1965)

> Try to include words or phrases from the documents in your answers.

D: The denial of the university really awakened even the politically dormant and inspired more questioning about the nature of the Northern state. 'The university decision' said [John] Hume 'electrified the people on the nationalist side and I think was really the spark that ignited the civil right movement... And when the university went to Coleraine, the chance of an orderly change in Northern Ireland probably disappeared. It became clear to me that change could only be effected by positive political action...' (from Frank Curran, *Derry: Countdown to Disaster*, Dublin, 1989, pp 42–3)

Comprehension

1   1 Which body issued Document C? What do you know about that body?

2   What does the body allege has been done in 'the past year or two'? List the five points it uses as evidence to support this allegation.

3   Who is quoted in Document D? What, in his opinion, were the results of the university decision?

Comparison

4   Is that opinion in Document D supported or undermined by Source C? Explain your answer by referring to information contained in the two documents.

Criticism

5   Which of the points mentioned in Document C seems to you to give most support to the nationalist claim that the decision to put the new university in Coleraine was a deliberate snub to the people living west of the Bann?

Contextualisation

5   What part did the controversy about the location of a second university for Northern Ireland play in nationalist attitudes to Terence O'Neill?

Timeline for Case Study

1961: Robins Committee on University Education in Britain.

1963: Terence O'Neill succeeds Lord Brookeborough as Prime Minister. Lockwood Committee established.

January-December 1964: Committee visits Queens, Derry and other sites. Discusses aspects of the question. Decides to recommend Coleraine as site for new university and closure of Magee.

December 1964: Northern Ireland Cabinet discusses report.

14 January 1965: Seán Lemass visits O'Neill in Belfast.

30 January 1965: Rumours about Lockwood decision led to founding of University for Derry Committee.

8 February 1965: Large all-party rally in Derry in support of the university.

9 February 1965: O'Neill visits Dublin.

10 February 1965: Lockwood Report published.

18 February 1965: Motorcade of 2000 vehicles goes to Belfast in protest. Two minute silence in Derry with many shops shut.

19 February 1965: O'Neill meets 'nameless, faceless men' in Derry.

March 1965: After 3 day debate, Stormont parliament accepts Report.

May 1965: Robert Nixon sparks off debate by claiming O'Neill was influenced by opposition of Derry Unionist leaders to developing the city in case it upset their control of the city.

(6) The Civil Rights Movement and the Fall of O'Neill

THE CHALLENGES FACING O'NEILL

By 1965 O'Neill faced challenges to his policies from two sides.

- Nationalists had hoped that his gestures towards them meant that he would support their claims to greater equality. But they were growing restless at the lack of real change.
- Extreme unionists resented even his gestures towards the nationalist community and began to campaign against him. The leading member of this campaign was a Protestant clergyman, the Reverend **Ian Paisley**.

THE CHANGING ATTITUDE OF YOUNGER NATIONALISTS

From the start, northern nationalists had opposed Northern Ireland. But by the 1960s some were tired of the futile whining of the Nationalist Party and the equally futile violence of the IRA. They were ready to try something new.

This was especially true of younger Catholics who had received a good education thanks to the reforms of the 1940s. In many ways they had done better there than they might have done in the South where educational opportunities were fewer. For them a united Ireland might be a dream but they knew it was not possible while one million unionists opposed it. They felt that if they were treated fairly they could settle down and work within Northern Ireland.

JOHN HUME

John Hume was typical of these people. For young northern nationalists like him in the 1960s a number of things created a sense of injustice. There was gerrymandering in local government, unfair allocation of houses, discrimination in jobs and the nature and attitude of the security services.

John Hume (1937–   ): Born in Derry in 1937, his family were poor because his father could not find work. Only with grants from the state could they afford to send him to secondary school and university. Hume became a teacher in Derry. He got involved in the local Credit Union which helped the poorest families and was one of the leaders in the campaign to get a university for Derry.

A crowded crumbling slum room, typical of many that Catholic families endured in Derry and other areas

GERRYMANDERING IN LOCAL COUNCILS

There were 73 local councils in Northern Ireland.

- Eleven were controlled by nationalists but they were all small urban councils like Newry or Strabane. They did not include any of the six county councils.
- Unionists controlled the remaining 62 local councils. Most were in areas east of the Bann where Protestants were in a clear majority and so it was natural that the unionists would be in a majority. They felt no need to gerrymander or to discriminate against Catholics in housing.
- The problem lay in 12 councils in border areas. In Fermanagh, Tyrone, Dungannon and above all in Derry city a majority of the people were Catholics but because of gerrymandering, Unionists had been in control since the early 1920s (see page 6).
- In Derry, for example, in 1967 the Unionist Party got 32 per cent of the vote but because of the way the wards were arranged, they got 60 per cent of the seats on the Corporation. This left them in control of the city.

HOUSES AND VOTES

Unionist control of local councils was helped by the **property qualification** for voting in local elections (see page 7). It continued in Northern Ireland long after it was abolished in the rest of the United Kingdom, because unionists feared that 'one person/one vote' might upset their control of gerrymandered councils, especially in Derry.

The property qualification applied equally to Catholics and Protestants. It therefore deprived poorer people from both communities of the chance to vote for the local councils which affected so many aspects of their lives. But as more Protestants than Catholics owned houses, the impact was greater on the Catholics.

The property qualification also had a big effect on the way that gerrymandered councils like Derry or Dungannon gave council houses to people living in slum conditions. Because giving someone a house also meant giving him/her a vote, these councils were understandably reluctant to give council houses to Catholics because that might upset their delicately balanced control.

In Derry (see page 6), for example, the Housing Trust which gave houses on a fair points system was only allowed to build in the overcrowded South Ward (which included the Catholic Bogside and the Creggan housing estate, see map on page 6). Houses in the more spacious North and Waterside Wards, where Protestants were in a majority, were built by the council and allocated only to Protestants.

Discrimination against Catholics in housing was not a problem in other areas of Northern Ireland. Overall Catholics made up 26 per cent of all households but they occupied over 30 per cent of all council houses. In Unionist-controlled Belfast, for example, 19 per cent of Catholics were in publicly owned houses compared with 9 per cent of Protestants. This was because in most places houses were given on a fair points system and Catholics tended to have bigger families and be poorer than Protestants.

DISCRIMINATION IN JOBS

For years Catholics claimed that they suffered discrimination in the allocation of jobs. This was especially clear in local government. Most councils, including those controlled by nationalists, favoured members of their own communities when giving out jobs. But since Unionists controlled 62 of the 73 councils, they had more jobs to give.

Unionists denied that they discriminated against Catholics. They pointed to statistics which showed that Catholics held about 30 per cent of local government and civil service jobs. That is roughly in proportion to their share in the population. That was true if all jobs were lumped together. Catholics had more than their fair share of lower paid, lower status jobs such as cleaners, gardeners or porters. But the picture changes if we look at higher paid jobs such as clerks, administrators or technicians.

Catholics felt especially bitter about the situation in the gerrymandered councils.

- In Derry, which was 60 per cent Catholic, only thirty per cent of administrative, clerical and technical staff were Catholic. A Southern Protestant reported in 1967 that '*of the heads of fifteen municipal departments, not one is a Roman Catholic. Of other senior Corporation officials, there is now a schools meals organiser who is a Catholic.*' (Terence de Vere White, 'A Stranger's Eye', Irish Times, 23 January 1967)
- In Dungannon, there was not one Catholic at that grade.
- In Fermanagh the Unionist-controlled council employed 338 Protestants and 32 Catholics – all as cleaners.

There was also evidence of job discrimination by the Stormont government.

- The Campaign for Social Justice reported in 1969 that of 319 top civil servants, only 23 (7.2 per cent) were Catholics.
- In 1969 there were six Catholics among the sixty-eight senior judges.
- O'Neill set up several important committees to enquire into social and economic issues without appointing a single Catholic to sit on them.
- In the publicly owned gas, electricity and water industries in 1971 only 1,952 workers (15.4 per cent) were Catholic.

- And of course the Unionist MPs and ministers who ran Northern Ireland were always exclusively Protestant.

THE RUC, THE B SPECIALS AND THE SPECIAL POWERS ACT

1 The Northern Ireland police force, the **Royal Ulster Constabulary** (RUC), was armed, unlike the police in Britain or the republic. In 1960 its numbers were limited to 3,500. Catholics generally distrusted the RUC and did not join it. As a result, it was about 90% Protestant and the few Catholics in it were not promoted to the higher ranks. Since the Unionist government often sent the RUC to take down nationalist flags or to protect Orangemen marching through nationalist areas, Catholics saw it as the armed servant of the Unionist state rather than a neutral police force.

2 The 'Specials Constables' had been set up to counter the IRA in 1920–22 but remained in existence after the threat was gone. At first there were 'A', 'B' and 'C' constables but by the 1960s only the **'B Specials'** remained. A heavily armed part-time force with about 8,500 men, it was exclusively Protestant. In rural areas, especially in the west, the B Specials patrolled country roads and often stopped and searched their Catholic neighbours. Their arrogance and their occasional firing on innocent people kept sectarian animosities alive.

3 Like the 'B Specials', the **Civil Authorities (Specials Powers) Act** was passed as a short-term measure against the IRA in 1921 but it was later made permanent. It allowed the Home Affairs Minister to order the arrest and detention of anyone, *who was acting, had acted or was about to act 'in a manner prejudicial to the preservation of peace and maintenance of order'*. The Act gave enormous powers to the Minister who could ban organisations he disliked or imprison people without trial (internment). Catholics noted bitterly that it was only used to ban nationalist demonstrations or organisations, never unionist ones.

PROTEST ABOUT HOUSING IN DUNGANNON

Since the 1920s Catholics had resented these injustices but it was only after O'Neill seemed to promise changes that they began to demonstrate against them. The first protests were against discrimination in housing.

In Dungannon, Co. Tyrone, in 1960 there were 300 Catholic families on the council's waiting list. Many of them lived in expensive, crowded and rat-infested private flats. In one house, eight couples and their children shared two cookers and two toilets. Dungannon council had built 194 houses in the previous 15 years but had consistently given most of them to Protestant families, often from outside the town.

Inspired partly by the black civil rights movement in America, forty young Catholic women drafted a petition to the council outlining their situation. When they did not get a response, they formed the **Homeless Citizens League** and began to picket council meetings. They were soon joined by **Patricia McCluskey** who, with her husband **Conn** a local doctor, began to collect evidence of discrimination in housing.

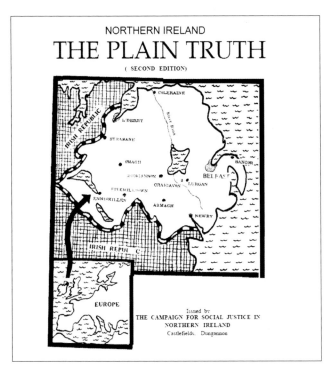

Patricia and Conn McCluskey felt that they could only gain attention for their cause if they produced facts to support their claims about discrimination

THE CAMPAIGN FOR SOCIAL JUSTICE (CSJ)

In January 1964 the McCluskeys helped to set up the **Campaign for Social Justice (CSJ)**. In a conscious break from the past, its members did not talk about partition or a united Ireland. Instead they concentrated on collecting facts about injustices to Catholics within Northern Ireland. In 1964 they published their findings in a pamphlet, *The Plain Truth* and presented them to prominent politicians in Westminster. They argued that if Northern Ireland was part of the United Kingdom then people living in it were entitled to the same rights as other UK citizens. They got a sympathetic hearing from Labour MPs and the Labour leader, Harold Wilson who had many Irish-born voters in his constituency near Liverpool.

> Conn and Patricia McCluskey were responsible for the formation of the Campaign for Social Justice that led to the formation of the Northern Ireland Civil Rights Association.

At the end of 1964 Labour won the British general election and Wilson became Prime Minister. But once in power he did not want to get drawn into the problems of Northern Ireland. He praised O'Neill's gestures towards nationalists and took refuge behind the Westminster convention that the London parliament did not discuss matters which were the responsibility of Stormont. Other Labour MPs were dissatisfied with this and in 1965 over 100 of them formed the **Campaign for Democracy in Ulster** to keep the pressure on the Unionist government.

IAN PAISLEY AND THE 'O'NEILL MUST GO' CAMPAIGN

But it would be difficult for O'Neill to deal with nationalist complaints. Even his very minor gestures towards them had aroused the anger of some in his own party and of **Ian Paisley** who emerged at this time as a leading figure on the northern scene.

This cartoon is typical of much of the media response to Paisley

Ian Paisley (6 April 1926–   ) Born in Lurgan in 1926, the son on a Baptist minister, Ian Paisley was ordained by his father in 1946. In 1951 he set up the **Free Presbyterian Church** of which he was the Moderator (head). A committed evangelical Protestant, he first came to prominence for staging protests against moves by the Church of Ireland and the Presbyterian Church to improve their relations with the Catholic Church (ecumenism) and against flags flying at half-mast to mark the death of Pope John XXIII in 1964.

Paisley was a powerful speaker with a flair for publicity. During the 1964 general election campaign he threatened to lead a mob to take down a tricolour flag flying in a nationalist area. When the RUC took it down instead, there were two days of rioting in which many people were hurt. He regularly staged protests against any gesture O'Neill made towards the Catholic community. He called him a 'Lundy', claimed he 'was not a Protestant' and began to use the slogan

'O'Neill must go'. These stunts attracted a great deal of attention from the media. Most of it was hostile but it won him a big following among rural and working-class Protestants who felt threatened by the changing economic and social conditions of the time.

The consequences of Paisley's campaign became clear in 1966 when nationalists celebrated the fiftieth anniversary of the Easter Rising. A group of extreme unionists in Belfast, calling themselves the **Ulster Volunteer Force**, saw the celebrations

Note: In is important not to confuse the **Presbyterian Church in Ireland** to which half of northern Protestants (about 500,000) belong with the **Free Presbyterian Church**. Set up by Ian Paisley and led by Ian Paisley it has about 30,000 members.

A cartoon from the late 1960s.

1   Who is the little man?

2   What message did the cartoonist intend to convey?

as a threat and decided to kill IRA men. They murdered three people, one an elderly Protestant woman, the others innocent Catholics. When arrested they claimed to have been inspired by Paisley, though he denounced their actions.

By 1967 the 'O'Neill must go' campaign had gained the support of a significant part of the Unionist party and the Orange Order. This made it very difficult for him to introduce reforms, just as nationalist demands for change grew louder.

GERRY FITT IN WESTMINSTER

Pressure for reform was also growing in Westminster. In the 1966 Westminster election Gerry Fitt stood as a Republican Labour candidate for the mainly nationalist constituency of West Belfast and was elected an MP.

Gerry Fitt (1926–2005) Born in Belfast and worked as a merchant seaman from 1941 to 1953. An active trade unionist, he was elected to Belfast Corporation and later to Stormont, before winning his Westminster seat.

An affable man, who was respected in the Labour movement, Fitt quickly became the most prominent spokesman for the nationalist community. From the start he ignored the Westminster convention of not discussing Northern Ireland. In speech after speech he attacked the injustices of the Unionist government. He was supported by sympathetic Labour MPs who asked why British taxpayers were subsidising a government which was responsible for so many injustices. Wilson called in O'Neill and other Unionist ministers but accepted their argument that reforms might destabilise Northern Ireland.

The Crooked Pillar

Fitt and the Civil Rights movement drew British attention to the situation in Northern Ireland, leading to comments like the one contained in this cartoon

Courtesy: British Cartoon Archive

THE NORTHERN IRELAND CIVIL RIGHTS ASSOCIATION (NICRA)

In 1967 frustration at the lack of reform from O'Neill led the foundation of the **Northern Ireland Civil Rights Association (NICRA)**. An umbrella movement rather than a party, it had a very mixed membership.

- There were moderate nationalists who included John Hume and the McCluskeys, as well as the conservative Nationalist Party. They just wanted full civil rights and an end to discrimination.
- There were some moderate unionists who believed the only security for Northern Ireland lay in justice for all its citizens.
- There were left-wing trade unionists, Labour party activists and communists who hoped for

Bernadette Devlin (23 April 1947–):
Born in Cookstown, Co Tyrone in 1947, she
took part in the first Civil Rights Association
marches. While studying in Queen's University
she was one of the founders of the radical
student movement, People's Democracy. She
unsuccessfully stood for the Stormont
Parliament in the election of February 1969
but in April won a by-election to Westminster
shortly before her 22nd birthday, making her
the youngest woman MP ever.

A poster showing a civil rights march. What do they ask for? What is not there?

Courtesy: Imagefile

a more socialist society. There were also
radical students who were influenced by the
wave of student militancy which swept across
Europe in 1967-68. The most prominent of
them was the young **Bernadette Devlin**.

- The IRA also supported NICRA. After the
failure of the 1950s border campaign, the
leadership in Dublin had decided to move away
from violence and to campaign on social issues.

Although some members of NICRA were unionist,
most came from the nationalist community. But
unlike earlier nationalists they did not talk about
partition. Instead, influenced by Martin Luther
King and the American civil rights movement, they
asked for just treatment within Northern Ireland.
Their demands included:

- An end to the Special Powers Act and the B
Specials,
- All council houses to be given on fair a points
system, and

- 'One man, one vote' in local elections and no
more gerrymandering.

THE UNIONIST RESPONSE TO NICRA

These were moderate demands but they were too
much for most unionists. They believed the
Special Powers Act and the B Specials were
necessary to protect them from the IRA, while
granting 'one man, one vote' would end Unionist
control of most councils west of the Bann. Instead
of considering reform, they claimed that NICRA
was part of a plot to overthrow Northern Ireland
and pointed to its republican and communist
members as proof of their claim.

AUGUST 1968: THE NICRA MARCH IN DUNGANNON

The first significant action in the campaign for civil
rights took place in Dungannon. **Austin Currie**, the
local Nationalist MP, encouraged two Catholic
families on the housing waiting list to squat in two
empty council houses. The RUC evicted them and
the local Unionist-controlled council then gave one
house to an unmarried Protestant girl.

Austin Currie (1939–   ) Born in Co Tyrone in 1939, he studied in Queen's and was elected to the Stormont Parliament as a nationalist MP in 1964. One of the original founders of the Civil Rights movement, he joined with other Stormont MPs to found the Social Democratic and Labour Party (SDLP) in 1970.

The incident attracted a lot of publicity and in August 1968 NICRA staged a protest march from Coalisland to Dungannon. Led by Currie and Fitt, the marchers did not use nationalist flags or slogans and instead sang the American civil rights anthem, 'We shall Overcome'. They planned to end with a meeting in the centre of Dungannon but on the eve of the march, Ian Paisley announced a counter demonstration there. Claiming to fear a riot, the RUC stopped the NICRA marchers going into the town. This set a pattern, repeated regularly over the next few years, in which a loyalist organisation could manipulate the police into banning a civil rights or nationalist demonstration.

OCTOBER 1968: THE CLASH IN DERRY

In Derry socialists like **Eamonn McCann** had already formed the Derry Housing Action Committee and launched a campaign against the housing policies of the Unionist council. After a series of protests which achieved both publicity and some limited success, McCann records that:

> ' ...our conscious, if unspoken, strategy was to provoke the police into overreaction and thus

spark off mass reaction against the authorities. We assumed that we would be in control of the reaction, that we were strong enough to channel it. The one certain way to ensure a head-on clash with the authorities was to organise a non-Unionist march through the city centre.' (Eamonn McCann, *War and an Irish Town*, Pluto Press, 1973, London, p. 91)

They persuaded NICRA to back a march on 5 October. They planned to go across the river and into the Diamond, the central square in Derry. The marchers picked this route to symbolise that their march was non-political and non-sectarian. But it would bring them right into the heart of the city whose Protestant inhabitants proudly remembered their ancestors' defiance of Catholic King James in 1688. For the Apprentice Boys this was an unbearable insult. They protested to the government that the Civil Rights movement was merely a cover for republicans and nationalists and announced on 1 October that they would also march on 5 October.

The Minister for Home Affairs was the hard-line **William Craig**. He seized on the Apprentice Boys' announcement as an excuse to ban their march and to forbid the NICRA marchers to go inside the walls of Derry. Moderates like Conn McCluskey and John Hume wanted to postpone the march for a week but McCann and the local radicals insisted on going ahead.

About 400 people turned up to march. They included Gerry Fitt and three British Labour MPs who came to watch. The RUC set up barricades, blocking the marchers. A few speeches were made, mostly calling for restraint. The crowd was peaceful until the police moved in, lashing out with their batons at men, women and children. Fitt was severely beaten around the head. TV cameras filmed the whole thing and within hours televisions in Britain and around the world were showing the events in Derry. After that, McCann concludes,

> ' ...a howl of elemental rage was unleashed across Northern Ireland, and it was clear that things were never going to be the same again.' (*War and an Irish Town*, 1973, Pluto Press, London, p. 95)

THE RESULT

This was a disaster for O'Neill and his government.

- The world's media suddenly focussed on Northern Ireland and began to ask questions about civil rights and Catholic grievances.

- In the nationalist community there was an explosion of anger. Seamus Heaney, noting that *'the new Londonderry air sounds very like 'We shall overcome'*, wrote: *'it seems now that the Catholic minority, if it is to retain any self-respect, will have to risk the charge of wrecking the new moderation and seeking justice more vociferously.'* (*The Listener*, 24 October, 1968).

- In Belfast radical students led by Bernadette Devlin and Michael Farrell set up the **Peoples' Democracy**. Influenced by Marxist ideas, they hoped to bring about a socialist revolution.

John Hume (left) and Ivan Cooper (right) of the Derry's Citizen's Action Committee with Gerry Fitt (centre), the West Belfast MP. They were in London in January 1969 taking part in a civil rights march to Downing Street

Courtesy: Getty

O'NEILL INTRODUCES SOME REFORMS

In London the Prime Minister, Harold Wilson, realised his previous policy of letting O'Neill bring in reforms at his own pace was no longer viable. He summoned O'Neill, Faulkner and Craig to Downing Street. There he and his Home Secretary **James Callaghan** who was the British minister with most responsibility for Northern Ireland threatened to cut British subsidies unless reforms were implemented.

O'Neill then produced a package of moderate reforms.

- They included a points system for council housing, an end to the business vote, a review of the Special Powers Act and a Development Commission to replace Derry city council.

- But they did not include 'one man, one vote'.

This was a mistake as it encouraged the civil rights campaign to continue while making many unionists think the issue was more important than it was. Many Unionist Party members, especially those west of the Bann, criticised O'Neill for giving in to London.

O'NEILL'S 'CROSSROADS' SPEECH

On 9 December, O'Neill appeared on television to ask the public for support. *'Ulster'* he told his audience *'is at a crossroads'*. He begged the civil rights movement to give time for the reforms to work, while pointing out to unionists that *'Northern Ireland's income is £200 million a year while we spend £300 million – only because Britain pays the balance'*.

The response was positive. People began to wear 'I back O'Neill' badges and NICRA promised to hold no more marches until mid-January. When Craig challenged O'Neill for giving in to British pressure, the Prime Minister felt strong enough to sack him.

THE PEOPLE'S DEMOCRACY MARCH

But the young activists in the People's Democracy were opposed to NICRA's moderation. As Marxists they hoped for a workers' revolution and naively believed that if they could overthrow the Unionist government, Protestant and Catholic workers would unite against capitalism.

Led by Michael Farrell, they planned a march from Belfast to Derry, starting on 1 January 1969. O'Neill let them go ahead with a small escort of RUC men. Paisley called on 'the loyal citizens of Ulster' to 'harass and harry' them and they came under attack as they walked through unionist areas. The worst episode was at **Burntollet Bridge** not far from Derry when 200 extreme unionists, including off-duty B Specials, attacked them with stones and clubs, leaving 13 marchers in need of hospital treatment. The episode was filmed and showed the RUC doing little to protect the marchers.

Riots broke out when they reached Derry. Youths from the Catholic Bogside threw stones at the police but when the RUC followed the rioters into the Bogside, a few constables *'were guilty of misconduct which involved assault ... malicious damage to property ... and the use of provocative sectarian and political slogans.'* (*The Cameron Report*, 1969, p 73) This undermined support for moderation among nationalists and Hume announced that NICRA marches would resume.

FEBRUARY 1969: O'NEILL CALLS AN ELECTION

Events were now slipping out of O'Neill's control. He quickly announced an enquiry into the causes of the violence. Chaired by Judge Cameron it produced the *Cameron Report* later that year. It criticised the behaviour of the RUC and many aspects of the Unionist government. A few days after the riots, Brian Faulkner, O'Neill's ablest minister resigned in protest and in February, twelve Unionist MPs demanded his resignation.

In a desperate attempt to show that the public supported him, O'Neill called an election for the

O'Neill narrowly defeats Paisley

Stormont parliament on 3 February. It was a confused campaign with pro- and anti-O'Neill Unionist candidates confronting each other. The results were mixed.

- Ian Paisley, who had set up the **Protestant Unionist Party**, stood against O'Neill in his own constituency and won 6331 votes to O'Neill's 7745.
- Overall 39 Unionist MPs were elected but only 27 of them were pro-O'Neill and the twelve who had challenged him all kept their seats.
- On the nationalist side several members of the civil rights campaign including John Hume won seats in Stormont, displacing members of the Nationalist Party which was almost wiped out. Bernadette Devlin stood for election but was defeated.

O'NEILL'S RESIGNATION

In March, O'Neill introduced a Public Order bill which outlawed many of the tactics used by the Civil Rights movement. This led to protests in Derry which on 19 April produced three days of riots between the RUC and youths from the Bogside. Poorly led and under great pressure, some RUC men were seen to be drunk and out of control. At one point they entered a house in the Bogside and beat the inhabitants, one of whom later died.

These disturbances overshadowed O'Neill's final decision on 22 April to bring in 'one man, one vote' in local elections. The move was condemned by the Apprentice Boys of Derry. **James Chichester Clarke,** the Minister for Agriculture, resigned in protest. A few days later bombs exploded in Belfast's water mains, creating an atmosphere of crisis. The RUC blamed republicans though it later emerged that the bombs were planted by loyalists who wanted to undermine O'Neill. He resigned.

ASSESSING O'NEILL

Most assessments of O'Neill stress his lack of warmth and skill in personal relationships.

- Having been brought up in England he lacked contact with ordinary unionists in Northern

Ireland and was not at ease with their customs and traditions.

- He also had few friends among Unionist MPs, even those who shared his views, so that when there was a crisis no one was prepared to take risks on his behalf.

- He found it impossible to convince most unionists of the need to modernise Northern Ireland, partly perhaps because like them, he tended to confuse genuine nationalist grievances with opposition to the existence of Northern Ireland or support for the IRA.

QUESTIONS

1 How were the attitudes of younger Catholics like John Hume towards Northern Ireland changing in the 1960s and what caused the change?

2 List the three main grievances that northern Catholics felt and explain each of them.

3 Where and how did the Civil Rights campaign begin?

4 List some of the groups involved in NICRA (Northern Civil Rights Association) and outline their demands. How did unionists respond to them?

5 Who led the 'O'Neill must go' campaign and why did it appeal to some unionists?

6 Describe the NICRA marches in Dungannon and Derry. What was the result of these marches?

7 How did (a) the British government and (b) O'Neill respond to these developments?

8 Outline the events which led from O'Neill's 'Crossroads Speech' to his resignation.

THE DESCENT INTO VIOLENCE

After O'Neill resigned, the Unionist Party, by 17 votes to 16, elected **James Chichester Clarke** rather than Brian Faulkner as its new leader. Like O'Neill, to whom he was related, Chichester Clarke came from the landed gentry and he shared O'Neill's lack of political skill. Unsuited to the task of restoring stability to Northern Ireland, he was in office for less than 18 months.

At first all seemed to be going well. Chichester Clarke promised to continue O'Neill's reform programme and announced an amnesty for offences committed during the riots. This had the advantage of freeing Ian Paisley who had been imprisoned for his part in a banned demonstration some months before. In return, NICRA called off further demonstrations. Although there was some rioting during the marching season nothing too serious happened until August.

James Chichester Clarke, the Prime Minister of Northern Ireland, visiting 10 Downing Street in 1969. Like O'Neill, he had to satisfy the British government that he was reforming Northern Ireland

Courtesy: Alamy

12 AUGUST 1969: THE 'BATTLE OF THE BOGSIDE'

In the Bogside the behaviour of the RUC earlier in the year had undermined support for moderate leaders like Hume. When the government decided to let the annual Apprentice Boys march go ahead in August, Bogsiders feared another RUC invasion. Young men began to stockpile stones and make petrol bombs.

On 12 August fifteen thousand Apprentice Boys arrived in Derry for their annual parade. At first it went peacefully until a few of the marchers threw pennies from the walls down onto the Bogside below. Young Catholics retaliated with stones and petrol bombs and soon a battle was raging. John Hume and Ivan Cooper tried to stop the violence but Bernadette Devlin urged the rioters to resist the RUC.

> **Petrol bomb:** a glass bottle is filled with petrol. The neck is stuffed with cloth and set alight just before it is thrown.

After two hours the RUC charged into the Bogside but had to retreat under a hail of stones and petrol bombs, thrown from the top of the ten-storey Rossville Flats. The police then fired clouds of CS gas which only strengthened the determination of the Bogsiders. Rioting continued for two days during which many RUC men were injured. To relieve the exhausted police, Chichester Clarke agreed to call in the B Specials. This only made things worse, as Catholics claimed that they sided with Protestant mobs.

CS Gas: A choking, blinding but harmless gas which was developed to help police stop riots. Later the RUC used 'plastic bullets' to control crowds. They were plastic batons about 6 inches long, which were fired from a special gun. Though less dangerous than real bullets they could cause death if they hit a person on the head.

Lynch's speech drew a hostile response from Unionists and the British.

1 What does the cartoon show him doing?
2 Was that a fair assessment of his speech?

JACK LYNCH'S SPEECH

In the republic people had watched the growing violence within Northern Ireland with dismay. The Fianna Fáil government was divided. Moderates who included the Taoiseach, **Jack Lynch**, wanted to avoid involvement while three ministers, Charles Haughey, Neil Blaney and Kevin Boland considered helping northern nationalists, possibly with guns.

The violence in Derry forced Lynch to do something. In a broadcast on 13 August he said that the South could *'no longer stand by and see innocent people injured and perhaps worse'*. Calling

for peace he promised to station Irish army hospital units along the border to help refugees.

The speech increased tension in the North. Nationalists hoped it meant he was sending in the Irish army to protect them while furious unionists feared that was his plan. In fact Lynch had no such intention. He knew very well that the Irish army had neither the men nor the equipment for such a task. Instead he hoped the British government would send in their army to separate the two sides.

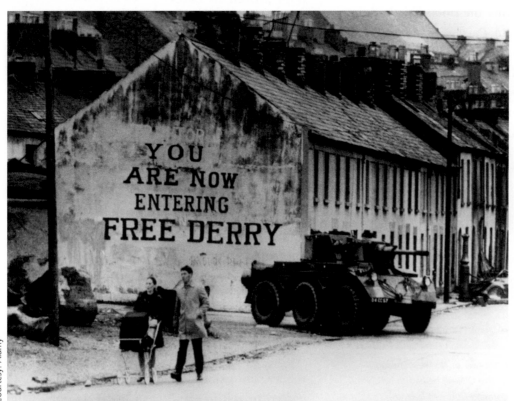

The Bogside of Derry became a 'no go' area for the RUC after the rioting of 1969. It was mainly controlled by the IRA

THE VIOLENCE SPREADS TO BELFAST

On the evening of 12 August, as the RUC charged into the Bogside, an appeal went out to nationalists elsewhere in the North to ease the pressure on Derry by organising demonstrations. The next day there were disturbances in half a dozen areas but the worst outbreak of violence took place in Belfast.

On 13 August there were riots in two Catholic areas, the Lower Falls and Ardoyne. On the following day when Catholics gathered again, a Protestant crowd, infuriated by the Lynch broadcast, appeared to challenge them. The RUC moved in to separate the two mobs. After the Catholics threw stones and petrol bombs, the police charged and drove them back into their own areas. The Protestant crowd followed accompanied, Catholics complained, by B Specials. After gunfire from the Catholic side, the police opened fire and the Protestant mob began burning Catholic houses and businesses. Four days of rioting followed, leaving seven people dead, five of them Catholic, and 180 premises burnt out, most of them Catholic-owned.

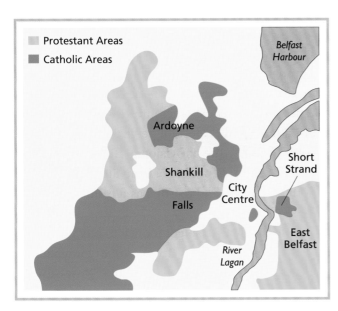

Location of key areas in Belfast

THE BRITISH ARMY ARRIVES

The spread of the riots showed that the exhausted RUC could no longer control the situation.

Chichester Clarke asked for help from the British army and Wilson and Callaghan agreed. British soldiers arrived in Derry on 14 August and in Belfast the following day. Catholics in both cities had felt under serious pressure and they welcomed the soldiers. Over the next few months the troops kept the peace. In Belfast this often meant allowing barricades to be put up separating Catholic areas from Protestant areas. At first these were made of barbed wire and burnt out cars but in time they became brick and concrete 'peace walls' which remained long after peace was restored. In the Bogside a barricade separated 'Free Derry' from the rest of Northern Ireland.

REFORM CONTINUED

The British government, not the Unionists, controlled the army and this drew them much more directly into the affairs of Northern Ireland. Callaghan came from London several times and made it clear to Chichester Clarke that his government could only survive if it continued to reform. Over the following months a series of important changes were put in place, fulfilling many of the aims of the Civil Rights movement.

- Local government was reorganised with fewer councils and an ombudsman to see fair treatment for all. Election to these councils was to be by PR and all citizens over 18 could vote.
- To prevent discrimination, the allocation of houses was taken from local councils and given to a **Housing Executive**.
- An English police officer was appointed as Chief Constable to reorganise the RUC. It was also decided that constables would no longer carry arms but this decision was later reversed.
- The B Specials were replaced by the **Ulster Defence Regiment** (**UDR**). It was to be part of the British army and have members drawn from both communities. The UDR was set up in 1970 and after the first year about a quarter of its members were Catholics.
- Loyalists in Belfast rioted when the reform of the RUC and the disbandment of the Specials were announced. During these riots they killed an RUC constable. He was the first policeman to die.

THE DEVELOPMENT OF PARAMILITARY ORGANISATIONS

Paramilitary organisations: Private organisations with some of the characteristics of an army.

The violence between the two communities and between them and the army and police provided a fertile ground for the growth of paramilitary organisations. The most important of them were the Provisional IRA and the Ulster Defence Association (UDA).

THE EMERGENCE OF THE PROVISIONAL IRA

In the 1960s the IRA's Dublin-based leaders were influenced by Marxist ideas and had moved from fighting partition to campaigning for civil rights. Many IRA men did not like this development or the Marxism of the leadership. They drifted away from the movement and sold their guns. By 1969 the IRA in Belfast had only around one hundred volunteers and twenty-four guns. When Protestant mobs attacked Catholic areas they were almost powerless to defend them. The words *IRA, I Ran Away*, appeared on walls and Belfast republicans resented their helplessness.

Republican: Originally this meant a person who wanted a republic but in Northern Ireland the word was usually used to describe nationalists involved in or supporting the use of force.
Nationalists usually meant moderates like members of the SDLP.

At an IRA convention in Dublin in December 1969 the leaders proposed that, for the first time, the IRA recognise the governments in Dublin and Belfast and let its elected representatives enter the Dáil and Stormont. This was too much for traditional republicans and the IRA split. A majority stayed with the leadership and they became known as the '**Official IRA**'. The minority elected a 'provisional executive' as a temporary measure and after that became known as the '**Provisional IRA**'. A similar split occurred in the republican party, Sinn Féin.

THE IDEOLOGY OF THE PROVISIONALS

The Provisionals held to the traditional republican doctrine. They believed:

- That the conflict in Northern Ireland was not between unionists and nationalists but between the British government who occupied Northern Ireland illegally and 'the Irish people' by which they meant either all the people living in Ireland or any Irish people who shared their views.
- That the purpose of the IRA was to drive the British out of Northern Ireland by force.
- That it was the British who stirred up sectarian conflict and prevented Irish unity.
- That if the British left, Protestant and Catholic would live happily together in a united Irish republic but if the Protestants did not, they could always 'go back to Britain'.

The Provisionals totally ignored the fact that a million Northern unionists considered themselves British and wanted to remain part of the United Kingdom. This made them a profoundly sectarian organisation and while they claimed to be fighting 'the British', in reality most of their victims were Northern Protestants.

THE PROVISIONALS GROW

Through the first half of 1970 frequent riots helped to increase support for both branches of IRA, especially in Belfast where there was a patchwork of Catholic and Protestant neighbourhoods side by side. In June, the Provisional IRA defended the Catholic Short Strand area from attack and gained both credibility and recruits as a result.

The Provisionals also got money to buy guns from Irish Americans and from some members of Fianna Fáil who preferred the Provisionals' traditional Catholic republicanism to the Marxism of the Official IRA.

JUNE 1970: A NEW GOVERNMENT IN BRITAIN

In June 1970 Wilson and the Labour party lost a general election in Britain and were replaced by the

Conservatives, led by **Edward Heath**. At first Catholics distrusted them because the Conservatives had traditionally been the allies of the Unionist Party. The new Prime Minister, **Edward Heath** and his Home Secretary, **Reginald Maudling**, had no previous experience of Northern Ireland and at first played a less active role than Callaghan. They were inclined to let the Unionist government and the British army commanders on the ground make the decisions. The result of this was seen in behaviour of the army during the Falls Road curfew.

3–5 JULY 1970: THE FALLS ROAD CURFEW HELPS THE IRA

Following a tip-off, the army found a cache of arms near the Catholic Falls Road on 3 July. After some stones were thrown at the soldiers, the army commander sent 3,000 troops to surround the Lower Falls area with armoured cars and helicopters. They imposed a 36 hour curfew which imprisoned about 20,000 people in their homes. Then soldiers went from a house to house, pulling up floor boards and smashing furniture as they searched for arms. They found over 100 guns. In an exchange of fire with the IRA, they killed four people, all Catholics. As a final insult, the army escorted two Unionist government ministers on a tour of the area after the curfew was lifted.

The 'Falls curfew' was a political disaster. It created the impression that the army was being used only against working class Catholics. Paddy Devlin recalled:

> 'Overnight the population turned from neutral to or even sympathetic support for the military to outright hatred of everything related to the security forces... Gerry Fitt and I witnessed voters and workers in the Dock and Falls constituencies turn against us to join the Provisionals.' (Paddy Devlin, *Straight Left*, The Blackstaff Press, Belfast 1993, p. 134)

After that the Provisionals felt strong enough to begin a bombing campaign. Their early targets were hotels, bus stations and other public utilities as well as the homes of prominent unionists. Their aim was to undermine the economy of Northern Ireland so that the British would leave.

A UFF flag flying from a lamp post in Belfast in 1973

Courtesy: Corbis

THE ULSTER DEFENCE ASSOCIATION (UDA)

As the violence spread, Protestants too sought to protect themselves by setting up loyalist paramilitary groups. Various local groups were formed to protect their districts from attack. In 1971 during the violence that followed internment (see below) some of them combined into the **Ulster Defence Association** (**UDA**). Its declared purpose was to defend Protestant areas from attack. At its height in 1971–73 it had about 40,000 members who manned barricades and patrolled their areas. A small group of UDA men, who often sheltered under the name of the **Ulster Freedom Fighters** (**UFF**), declared their intention of killing republicans. In practice, however, most of their victims were unfortunate Catholics who crossed their path by chance. In 1972–73 they killed over 200 people.

> **Loyalists:** Originally this meant all unionists but it gradually changed to mean only those unionists who were involved in paramilitary organisations.

THE MODERATE MAJORITY

Not many people from either community were involved in paramilitary groups. Most Catholics and Protestants remained loyal to the idea of democratic politics and supported parties opposed to violence.

FOUNDING THE SOCIAL DEMOCRATIC AND LABOUR PARTY

Among nationalists, the old Nationalist Party had lost credibility during the civil rights campaign. In the 1969 election it lost three of its Stormont seats to Independents associated with NICRA, John Hume, Ivan Cooper and Paddy O'Hanlon. In Belfast Gerry Fitt was elected for Republican Labour and Paddy Devlin for the NILP.

These results left the nationalist community without a party to speak on its behalf to the government in London. To provide one, John Hume worked to unite anti-unionist MPs. He easily got the support of **Cooper**, **O'Hanlon** and the Nationalist MP **Austin Currie** but like Hume himself they represented nationalist areas west of the Bann. To be credible, the new party also needed to represent working class Catholics from Belfast. This was achieved when **Gerry Fitt** of Republican Labour and **Paddy Devlin** of the NILP agreed to join them. But they insisted that the new party's name must include the word 'labour'.

> **What's in a name?**
> Fitt wanted the party to be called the Labour and Social Democratic Party but gave up the idea when Devlin pointed out that it would be the LSD Party!

In August 1970 the **Social Democratic and Labour Party** (**SDLP**) was set up. Fitt was chosen as leader because he was the oldest and most experienced and, as a Westminster MP, had good contacts with British leaders. Hume, better educated and more interested in ideas than Fitt, was deputy leader.

The SDLP promised:

- to work for co-operation between nationalists and unionists within Northern Ireland and
- to build bridges between North and South in the hope that Ireland would eventually be reunited with the consent of the Protestant majority.

The SDLP claimed it was not a sectarian party but although one of its founders, Ivan Cooper, was a Protestant it failed to persuade Protestants to vote for it and remained the voice of moderate Catholic nationalists.

From the start there were tensions in the party. The MPs from west of the Bann represented rural or middle-class Catholics for whom nationalism was an important issue. Fitt and Devlin, on the other hand, represented urban working-class people mainly in Belfast for whom social issues like redundancy and unemployment were more important. They also lived in majority Protestant areas and were more sensitive to unionist fears than the more secure Catholics of the west and south.

THE IDEA OF POWER-SHARING

By the time the SDLP was set up most of the aims of the original civil rights campaign had been achieved and John Hume began to consider what policy the SDLP should adopt.

- Its ultimate aim was to end partition but unionist opposition meant that could not happen for a long time. Meanwhile, the SDLP could be condemned to permanent and futile opposition.
- Hume argued that this reflected the unfair way Northern Ireland had been set up with over 60 per cent of the population Protestant. As long as people voted along sectarian lines, the Catholic minority would always be excluded from a say in the way their state was run.
- To overcome this inbuilt injustice, Hume argued that some way must be found to allow the two communities to **share power** between them.

THE ALLIANCE PARTY

A similar idea lay behind the formation of another new party in April 1970. Called the **Alliance Party**, its founders hoped to create a non-sectarian party which both Catholics and Protestants could support. Most of its early members were liberal unionists who hoped to encourage people from both communities to work together for the good of all. But the success of Alliance was limited by the fact that it supported the Union with Britain and so was not attractive to nationalists. Over the years its support hovered at around 10 per cent of voters. But even this enabled it to play an important role in the formation of power-sharing governments.

QUESTIONS

1 Who was James Chichester Clarke and how did he become Prime Minister of Northern Ireland? What did he promise to do?

2 Why did violence erupt in Northern Ireland in August 1969? Give a brief account of the events that brought British soldiers onto the streets?

3 Name four important reforms that were introduced in 1969-70 and briefly explain each.

4 Write a page on the Provisional IRA explaining (a) why they were formed, (b) what they believed and (c) why they grew so quickly.

5 Name the main loyalist paramilitary group and explain its origin and policies.

6 Which party won the British general election in June 1970? Name two of its leaders and say what their attitude towards Northern Ireland was.

7 Write a brief account of the Social Democratic and Labour Party explaining
(a) why it was founded
(b) who its members were and
(c) what it hoped to achieve.

8 What was the Alliance party? Why was it important?

THE SEARCH FOR
NEW BEGINNINGS
1971–1974

CHICHESTER CLARKE RESIGNS

Throughout 1970 Chichester Clarke pushed ahead with his reforms. **Brian Faulkner**, who now recognised that change was necessary, backed him but he was opposed by **William Craig**. Craig had the support of many Unionist Party members, especially those from west of the Bann. They felt let down by the changes in local government and the

loss of the B Specials whom they regarded as their defenders against republicans. They wanted the army to get tough on the IRA, intern its leaders and reoccupy nationalist 'no-go' areas like 'Free Derry'.

After the Falls Road curfew, violence continued through the winter and spring of 1970-71. Early in 1971 the Provisional IRA blew up a BBC transmitter near Enniskillen, killing five men who were working on it. On 10 March they kidnapped three Scottish soldiers who were having an off-duty drink and murdered them. Two of them were brothers aged seventeen and eighteen. Horror at this brutality sent Chichester Clarke to London to ask Heath for tougher action against the IRA. When the request was refused he resigned.

Cummings

This cartoon shows that IRA actions like the killing of three off duty soldiers reduced sympathy for Northern Catholics and strengthened support for Unionists

Courtesy: British Cartoon Archive

23 MARCH 1971: BRIAN FAULKNER BECOMES PRIME MINISTER

Craig sought the leadership of the Unionist Party but it elected **Brian Faulkner** instead. More able and professional than O'Neill or Chichester Clarke, he tried to strike a balance between the demands of ordinary unionists for tougher action and the demands of the British for concessions to the nationalists.

- He gave a post in his Cabinet to a member of the Northern Ireland Labour Party, the first time a non-Unionist had been included.
- He offered the SDLP a limited form of power-sharing. The Stormont parliament would set

up five committees to oversee certain areas of government and members of the opposition would chair two of them.

- He banned all marches across Northern Ireland, much to the annoyance of the Orange Order.
- But he also got the British government to agree to a tougher security policy including the right of soldiers to fire on rioters.

At first the SDLP entered discussions with Faulkner about his Committees idea. But in July, after the army shot two innocent men during a riot in Derry, it demanded an enquiry. When Faulkner refused, SDLP MPs withdrew from Stormont.

DECIDING ON INTERNMENT

Faulkner thought that the best way to end violence was to **intern** leaders of the IRA. In the 1950s he had used internment to stop the IRA's border campaign and he believed it would work again. After it, with peace restored, he hoped moderate political leaders could enter into talks.

Increasing violence helped Faulkner to get Heath and Maudling to agree. Up to July there had been over 300 bomb explosions, most though not all, by the Provisional IRA. Then in July, to mark the Orange marching season, the Provisionals launched a major bombing campaign. If nothing was done, both Faulkner and the British feared a Protestant backlash with loyalists taking matters into their own hands.

> **Internment:** a policy of rounding up people suspected of violence and imprisoning them without trial for as long as was needed to restore peace. Both Irish governments used internment against the IRA during World War II and again in the 1950s.

9 AUGUST 1971: INTERNMENT FAILS

From 4 am on 9 August soldiers, accompanied by RUC Special Branch officers, raided houses across Northern Ireland. By 7.30 am they had seized over 340 men and taken them to holding centres to await interrogation.

It quickly became clear that the whole operation was a disaster.

- The RUC lists of IRA members were seriously out of date. Most of the men arrested were either innocent or had long since retired from active involvement in the IRA. Within three days 140 of them were freed but some were so angry at the casual brutality of the soldiers who arrested them that they joined the IRA.
- Most of the current IRA leaders escaped arrest, either because the RUC did not know who they were or because they suspected internment was coming and stayed away from home.

"I think your first task is to stop the wall going any higher!"

This cartoon shows what the British expected of Faulkner

Courtesy: British Cartoon Archive

FÜHRER FAULKNER WANTS YOU FOR HIS CONCENTRATION CAMPS!

Internment gave the IRA a wonderful opportunity for propaganda. What message does this leaflet try to give?

Courtesy: CAIN (cain.ulst.ac.uk)

- Worst of all from the point of view of community relations, internment was completely one-sided. Not a single loyalist was arrested although they too were involved in riots and murder. The handful of Protestants who were rounded up had been active in the civil rights campaign, not in paramilitary violence.
- The arrests continued for several months. By the end of the year over 2,000 had been taken in, although most were freed within days.

TORTURE?

> The government later built new prison blocks, shaped like the letter H at **Long Kesh** and renamed it **The Maze** to improve its image.

Internees were lodged in a ship moored in Belfast Lough or in rusting nissen huts at an old army camp at **Long Kesh**. Conditions for prisoners were bad and reports soon emerged that about a dozen of them had been beaten, hooded, forced to stand for long periods and deprived of food and drink. The British dismissed these reports but journalists uncovered too many cases to be ignored. Eventually the Irish government took a case to the European Court of Human Rights which condemned their treatment as 'inhuman and degrading' though not quite torture.

A VIOLENT REACTION

Internment unleashed a new wave of violence, worse than anything seen before.
- Rioting and gun battles between the troops and both IRAs erupted across the North. On 10 August 1971 alone, eleven people died in Belfast and over 400 houses were burnt.
- The number of deaths rose sharply. In 1971 between 1 January and 9 August, 34 people died; from 9 August to 31 December the death toll was 150.
- The Provisional IRA gained support and manpower, which increased its ability to shoot and bomb.
- Loyalist vigilante groups set up the UDA and set out to kill republicans, which often turned out to mean innocent Catholics.

An anti-internment poster from 1971

Courtesy: CAIN (cain.ulst.ac.uk)

THE IMPACT OF THE VIOLENCE

Both communities suffered from the violence that followed internment but the impact was greatest on Catholics in the working class areas of Belfast and Derry.
- Almost half of the 150 who died in the months after internment were Catholics.
- Twenty-nine of them were killed by the British army. Many were innocent civilians, though in most cases the army insisted they were gunmen. This angered their relatives and neighbours.
- 7,000 Catholics fled for safety to the South while several hundred Protestants sought refuge in Britain.
- About 1,000 Catholic families and 750 Protestant families moved from their homes in mixed housing estates to areas where they felt safer. It was the biggest movement of population in Europe since the end of World War II.
- This greatly increased the share of the northern population which lived in segregated ghettos. Barricades, later transformed into permanent 'peace walls', separated and protected the inhabitants of the ghettos from each other.

ATROCITIES

It seemed to many in the Catholic ghettos that both the RUC and the British army were attacking rather than defending them. They therefore turned to the Provisional IRA for protection. The Provisional IRA grew in numbers and confidence and came to believe it was winning. This encouraged it to continue its bombing campaign. Loyalists retaliated, though they used assassination more often than bombs.

Two examples from Belfast show the result:
- On 4 December 1971 a bomb blew up McGurk's crowded bar, killing 15 people. Rescue workers used their bare hands to dig the dead and injured from the collapsed building. At first the RUC and the army claimed it was an IRA bomb that had gone off early but it soon became clear that it was planted by the UVF.
- On 11 December a republican bomb in a furniture store on the Protestant Shankill road killed two adults and two children.

PEACEFUL PROTESTS

In the South, Jack Lynch had advised the British against internment and he protested to Heath about the way it was carried out. Sympathy for northern Catholics grew and money was collected to help the families of men who had been interned.

The SDLP denounced both internment and the violence that followed. To channel nationalist anger into peaceful protest, they:
- urged nationalists to withdraw from local councils and organisations like the Ulster Defence Regiment,
- supported a rent and rates strike and
- organised marches and demonstrations, even though these had been illegal since before internment.

> **Rent strike:** council tenants would not pay rents.
>
> **Rates strike:** property owners would not pay local taxes (rates) to councils.

Outside the ghetto areas most nationalists supported these peaceful protests and were appalled by the indiscriminate violence of the IRA.

A poster supporting the rent and rates strike

Courtesy: CAIN (cain.ulst.ac.uk)

DERRY BEFORE BLOODY SUNDAY

In 1971, Derry with its nationalist majority saw less violence than Belfast. After internment, moderate nationalists got the British army to agree not to go into the Bogside and Creggan areas where 33,000 mainly working class Catholics lived. They hoped this would keep the peace but it did not. The IRA used the 'no go areas' as safe havens from which they could shoot at British troops. In January 1972 there were over 80 shooting incidents and IRA snipers killed two soldiers.

Among the inhabitants of the Bogside and the nearby Creggan estate unemployment was as high as 50 per cent and there were many young men with time on their hands. The presence of the British army provided them with a dangerous but stimulating outlet for their energies. Every night they headed towards the city centre to throw petrol bombs, nail bombs and stones at the troops who replied with CS gas and plastic bullets. Sometimes the youths, whom the army called the **Young Derry Hooligans** (**YDH**), acted as decoys, drawing the soldiers who followed them within the reach of IRA snipers. Then people got killed in the crossfire.

Courtesy: Getty

British soldiers rounding up young men after the shooting

30 JANUARY 1972: BLOODY SUNDAY

By January, General Ford, who was in charge of the army in Northern Ireland, had decided to take action against the Young Derry Hooligans, perhaps even shooting some of 'the ringleaders'. When the local RUC commander, who happened to be a Catholic, protested at these plans, Ford ignored him and there is no evidence that he asked Heath in London or Faulkner in Belfast for approval. He drafted in the Parachute Regiment to supplement other soldiers on the ground. The 'Paras' had been trained to fight with maximum force; they were totally unsuitable for crowd control.

Ford's opportunity came when the Civil Rights movement organised an illegal anti-internment march for Sunday 30 January. Both Official and Provisional IRAs claimed later that they told their members who attended to leave their guns at home. About 15,000 people turned up and as the troops shepherded the crowd through the city streets, youths pelted the soldiers with missiles.

Then Ford ordered the Parachute Regiment into action. It fired 180 rounds into the crowd. Later the soldiers claimed that someone had fired on them first but no one in the crowd heard any other shots, no guns were found on any of the victims and no soldier was injured. When the shooting stopped one woman and 12 men were wounded and 13 men were dead, seven of them under nineteen years of age. The Derry coroner noted

later that many were shot in the back and added '*I say without reservation it was sheer, unadulterated murder*'. (Jonathon Bardon, *A history of Ulster*, Belfast, 2001, p. 688)

THE IMPACT OF BLOODY SUNDAY

Like internment, the Derry killings made things worse.

- In Derry itself, the number joining the Provisional IRA grew rapidly as young people sought revenge for the killings. Father Edward Daly who was there and tended the wounded said: '*in later years, many of the young people I visited in prison told me quite explicitly that they would never have become involved in the IRA but for what they witnessed and heard of happening on Bloody Sunday*'. (David McKittrick and David McVea, *Making Sense of the Troubles*, Penguin, London, 2001)
- Across the North, nationalists demonstrated in protest and John Hume said on RTÉ that many in Derry '*feel now it's a united Ireland or nothing*'.
- In the South, Jack Lynch recalled the Irish ambassador from London and declared a day of mourning. Public anger was expressed in protest marches and during one on 2 February a mob burnt down the British Embassy.
- In London, when Reginald Maudling told the House of Commons that the British soldiers had fired in self-defence, Bernadette Devlin ran across to hit him in the face.

Paratroopers arresting a young man on Bloody Sunday

Bernadette Devlin's action got almost as much attention in Britain as Bloody Sunday

'Of course, some innocent civilians become victims.'

By the time the Widgery Report appeared, Stormont was suspended and William Whitelaw was ruling Northern Ireland. As this cartoon suggests, it did little to help his delicate balancing act

THE WIDGERY REPORT

The London government quickly set up an enquiry, chaired by **Lord Chief Justice Widgery**. He interviewed soldiers and people who had been on the march. He concluded that, while no guns had been found *'there is a strong suspicion that some* [of those killed] *had been firing weapons or handling bombs'* and that, at worst, some of the soldiers' firing *'bordered on the reckless'*.

Nationalists were outraged. They called the Widgery Report a whitewash, which was intended to protect the reputation of the British army. Families of the dead continued to agitate for the next thirty years to have the case reopened.

BOMBS

Violence bred violence:

- In February the Official IRA set off a bomb in the London headquarters of the Parachute Regiment. It killed a Catholic priest, a gardener and five women who worked in the canteen.
- In March the Provisionals bombed the Abercorn, a popular restaurant in central Belfast which was crowded with Saturday shoppers. Two young women died and seventy people were injured. One was a girl who was soon to be married. She lost both legs, an arm and an eye. Her sister lost both legs.
- Two weeks later a 200-pound bomb went off in Belfast city centre. Contradictory warnings were given so that some of the crowd ran into the path of the bomb. Over 150 people were injured.

SEEKING A NEW POLICY

Up to Bloody Sunday, the British Prime Minister, Edward Heath, had backed Faulkner in the hope that his policy of internment might eventually bring peace. Bloody Sunday and its violent aftermath showed it would not and the British government began to look for an alternative policy.

They considered a range of options:

- **Repartition**, with majority Catholic areas going to the republic. This was rejected because it would have meant moving thousands of people from one part of Northern Ireland to another.
- **Reunification** with the south. This was rejected because talks with Lynch made it clear that however much the Republic's leaders might talk about ending partition, they could not afford to take on the North.
- **Joint authority**, with the Republic and Britain both responsible for governing the North. This was rejected as being unacceptable to Protestants.
- In the end, Heath came to the conclusion that the only way to restore and guarantee peace was to offer the Catholic minority a permanent role in the government of Northern Ireland ('**power-sharing**'). To reassure unionists that they would not be forced into a united Ireland against their will, there would be regular referendums ('**border polls**') in which the voters could choose either Union with Britain or a united Ireland.

23 MARCH 1972: THE END OF STORMONT AND THE START OF DIRECT RULE

Faulkner continued to insist that internment was working but the British did not believe him. At a meeting on 22 March they told him they planned to invoke Article 75 of the Government of Ireland Act and take complete control of security within Northern Ireland. When the Unionist ministers heard this, they resigned. Heath at once appointed **William Whitelaw** to be the Secretary of State for Northern Ireland. After 50 years, **devolved government** in Northern Ireland had been replaced by **direct rule** from London.

> **Devolved government:** A Belfast-based government dealing with Northern Ireland issues, and overseen by the British.
> **Direct rule:** The British government ruling Northern Ireland directly from London.

UNIONIST DIVISIONS

These were traumatic events for ordinary unionists.
- The reforms forced on them by London robbed them of power.
- The ending of the B Specials took away their protection.
- Now the end of Stormont left them at the mercy of a British government which, it was rumoured, had considered Irish reunification.

The once united unionists began to fragment as they argued about what to do next.

WILLIAM CRAIG AND VANGUARD

Shortly after Bloody Sunday, William Craig set up **Ulster Vanguard**, as what he called a 'third force'. On 18 March at a rally attended by 60,000 people, he said: *'We will not accept direct rule .... If the politicians fail, it will be our job to liquidate the enemy'.* When Heath imposed direct rule he organised a two day general strike which cut

William Craig (1924–   ) Born in Cookstown, Co Tyrone in 1924, he was elected to the Stormont parliament in 1960. As Minister for Home Affairs in 1968 he opposed the Civil Rights movement, believing it to be a front for the IRA and banned several of its marches, including the 5 October march in Derry which sparked off the violence. After O'Neill sacked him in December he began to develop his own Vanguard movement.

transport and electricity supply by a third. Craig also argued that Northern Ireland should seek independence from Britain rather than submit to rule from London.

But although Vanguard looked formidable at first, it had only a limited appeal. Craig's violent language and his links with loyalist paramilitaries, who stewarded his meetings, frightened off middle class Protestants while many in the working class feared that an independent Northern Ireland without British subsidies would have nothing to offer them.

IAN PAISLEY AND THE DEMOCRATIC UNIONIST PARTY (DUP)

In 1972 Ian Paisley was less influential than Craig but he was a more astute politician. By then he was an MP in both Stormont and Westminster but many Protestants were put off by the crude anti-

Catholicism of his Protestant Unionist Party. This began to change, partly through his experience at Westminster where such naked sectarianism was unacceptable and partly through his friendship with a unionist lawyer, Desmond Boal. Boal encouraged Paisley to appeal to the Protestant working class, especially in Belfast. They had never felt that the old Unionist party, with its upper-class, often rural leaders, really represented them.

In 1971, as part of this programme, Paisley replaced the Protestant Unionist Party with the **Democratic Unionist Party (DUP)**. Unlike Faulkner's Ulster Unionist Party (UUP), the DUP was tightly disciplined, with one undisputed leader and a band of devoted party workers, many drawn from Paisley's own Free Presbyterian Church. Paisley's first response to direct rule was to propose that Northern Ireland be more fully integrated into the United Kingdom. This was never a popular policy and he gradually abandoned it in favour of the restoration of devolved government.

THE UNIONIST PARTY AFTER DIRECT RULE

The once mighty UUP suffered badly from direct rule:

- It lost members with moderates going to the Alliance Party on one side and hard-liners to Vanguard or the DUP on the other.
- For fifty years it had formed the government of Northern Ireland and its leaders were able to rely on civil servants for research and advice. Now overnight this had changed and the leaders had to build a back-up staff from scratch.
- It also lacked a strong central organisation. Party leaders did not control its governing body, the **Ulster Unionist Council**, which contained representatives of other organisations like the Orange Order. Neither did they control the local constituencies which could pick any candidate they liked for an election.

NATIONALISTS AND DIRECT RULE

For nationalists, direct rule seemed a hopeful development:

- Moderates like the SDLP rejoiced in the end of Unionist rule and hoped for peace and power-sharing.
- The extremists in the IRA saw it as a victory for their violent campaign. They thought that more violence would drive out the British and create a united Ireland. After a meeting to consider what their response should be, they announced: *'the war goes on'*.

QUESTIONS

1. Write a short account of Brian Faulkner's career before he became Prime Minister. List three things he did when he came to power.

2. Explain the meaning of 'internment'. Why was it introduced in Northern Ireland in 1971 and why did it fail?

3. Do you think internment made things better or worse? Explain your answer by referring to developments in the weeks that followed.

4. Why did 'Bloody Sunday' in Derry happen and what were its results?

5. What was the response of the British government to developments in Northern Ireland between March 1971 and March 1972?

6. How did unionists respond to the imposition of direct rule from London?

7. How did nationalists respond to direct rule?

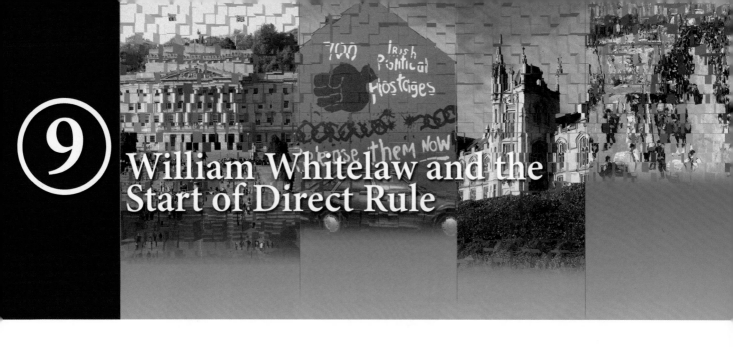

⑨ William Whitelaw and the Start of Direct Rule

WILLIAM WHITELAW

William Whitelaw was the first **Secretary of State for Northern Ireland** under direct rule. A leading English Conservative, he knew little about the area he now had to govern. Faulkner later wrote of him:

> 'He came armed with the wrong ideas about our problems and his policies for the first four months were an almost unmitigated disaster. But he had a priceless asset in his personality. He was a large, genial and humane man, deeply affected by the suffering of others but possessing the necessary sense of humour to allow him to survive in Northern Ireland. He laughed deafeningly at things which amused him... I rapidly gained a personal respect for Willie. He was a well meaning-man doing what he thought was best in very difficult circumstances.' (Brian Faulkner, *Memoirs of a Statesman*, London, 1978, p. 160)

Whitelaw knew he must win the trust of the Catholic community. To do that he planned to:

- restrain the British army,
- phase out internment and
- see if he could persuade the IRA to end its violence.

But he also knew he must not alienate the Protestants so he had to:

- restore order and
- get police back into the 'no-go' areas from which the IRA launched much of its violence.

Once he had restored peace, he then hoped to guarantee future stability by creating a new constitutional framework that would give the minority community a role in the government of Northern Ireland (i.e. power-sharing).

VIOLENCE GOES ON

Both wings of the IRA saw the fall of Stormont as a victory for them. One more push, they believed, could bring about Irish unity. They stepped up their violence.

William Whitelaw was a senior member of the Conservative government in London when Heath sent him to Belfast as the first Northern Secretary

Courtesy: Getty

"It's up to you, Willie. The whole world is watching."

Look closely at this cartoon.

1 Who is speaking?
2 Who is 'Willie' and what has he to do?
3 This is an British cartoon. What attitude does it show towards the Northern problems? Explain your answer.

- On 14 April 1972 alone the Provisionals set off 30 bombs across the North.
- Loyalists retaliated with bombs and riots but also by torturing and killing individual Catholics who crossed their path.
- Riots continued. People were killed in crossfire between the army or loyalists and the IRA. Car bombs killed innocent passers-by from both communities. In May there were 40 deaths, the highest total for any month to date.

Some of the dead were women and children, the very people the paramilitaries claimed to be defending. This led to a demand for peace, even in the Catholic ghettoes. In Belfast, women peace workers collected 50,000 signatures on a petition calling on both wings of the IRA to put aside their arms. On 29 May 1972 the Official IRA called a ceasefire but the Provisionals still refused. Their leaders, especially in the North, feared that a truce would undermine the will to go on fighting.

DEALING WITH INTERNMENT

Whitelaw tried to foster peace.
- He released hundreds of internees. After a hunger strike in June, he gave 'special category status' to those who remained. That meant treating them more like prisoners of war than ordinary criminals – they could wear

their own clothes, did not have to work and had more visits and parcels.
- He set up an enquiry under Lord Diplock to find other ways of dealing with people accused of political crimes. As a result of Diplock's enquiry, the discredited Special Powers Act was replaced by the **Northern Ireland (Emergency Provisions) Act** in August 1973.
- The act gave the RUC and the army extensive powers to question, search, arrest and detain people they suspected of violence.
- It also introduced the so-called **Diplock Courts** in which one judge, sitting without a jury, tried political cases. This was necessary as terrorist groups could easily intimidate jury members.

TALKS WITH THE PROVISIONALS FAIL

Whitelaw also encouraged John Hume to talk to the Provisionals. This finally led to a ceasefire on 26 June. On 7 July, six leading Provisionals were secretly flown to London. They included the Dublin-based **Seán MacStiofáin**, **Gerry Adams** from Belfast who was released from detention to attend and the IRA's Derry commander, **Martin McGuiness**. When they met Whitelaw they demanded:
- that all remaining detainees be freed and
- that Britain promise to leave Northern Ireland within three years.

The British, used to compromise and negotiation, found Northern Ireland's politicians' refusal to talk hard to understand

Whitelaw told them these were 'impossible demands'. He pointed out to them that the 1949 Ireland Act committed the British to keeping Northern Ireland in the United Kingdom as long as the majority there wanted it.

The Dublin-based IRA leaders wanted the ceasefire to continue but the Northerners, especially Adams, feared it would let the British army gain the upper hand. When rioting flared up between Protestant and Catholic areas in Belfast on 9 July, the local Provisionals opened fire and violence resumed.

21 JULY 1972: BLOODY FRIDAY

Over the next few days, furious fighting killed ten people. Then on Friday 21 July the full viciousness of the Provisionals car bomb campaign was made clear.

It was a fine day so many people went shopping in the centre of Belfast. Around 2.00pm bomb warnings began. At 2.10pm a huge bomb demolished the bus station which had been cleared. Over the next thirty minutes three more bombs destroyed a hotel, a railway station and government tax offices. So far there were only minor injuries. Then at 2.48pm a bomb destroyed another bus depot. It killed two soldiers and four

For more information on 'Bloody Friday' see http://cain.ulst.ac.uk/events/bfriday/

other people. Rescuers had to scrape up *'the remains of human beings into plastic bags like lumps of red, jellied meat from the pavement'* (Alf McCreary, *Survivors*, Belfast, 1976, p. 144).

Over the next half hour there were twelve more explosions around the city. They killed three more people and left 130 people seriously injured. One of the dead was a fourteen-year-old boy whose father, a clergyman, went to help the wounded, unaware of his son's death. As well as actual bombs, dozens of hoax warnings spread terror among the thousands of frightened people trying to get home on foot along blocked roads and ruined railways.

Three large bombs also exploded in Derry and another sixteen in other areas. In addition another five people were shot as the Provisionals engaged in fierce gun battles with the British troops.

'OPERATION MOTORMAN' AND THE BOMBING OF CLAUDY

'Bloody Friday' aroused horror throughout Ireland. No cause could justify this slaughter of the innocent. Whitelaw took advantage of the outrage to launch **'Operation Motorman'** to end the 'no go' areas in Derry and Belfast. Extra troops were poured in to the North and at dawn on 30 July they began to dismantle the barricades. In a show of even-handedness, the Parachute Regiment was sent to deal with barriers in loyalist areas.

There was little direct resistance but on 31 July the Provisionals retaliated. They left three car bombs in the mixed and peaceful village of Claudy near Derry. A warning was phoned but it was too late. The first bomb had already gone off and people fleeing from it ran into the path of the others. Nine died, five Protestants and four Catholics, and thirty were horribly injured. The Provisional IRA did not claim responsibility but everyone knew who did it.

The poet James Simmons expressed a deeply felt outrage in his poem *Claudy*. It begins by describing a normal peaceful morning in the village, then

An explosion too loud for your ear drums to bear
And young children are squealing like pigs in the square,
And all faces chalk white and streaked with bright red
And the glass and the dust and the terrible dead

For an old lady's legs are ripped off and the head
Of a man's hanging open and still he's not dead.
He is screaming for mercy and his son stands and stares
And stares then suddenly, quick, disappears.

And Christ, little Katherine Aitkins is dead
And Mrs McLoughlin is pierced through the head.
Meanwhile to Dungiven the killers have gone
And they're finding it hard to get through on the phone.
(Frank Ormsby, *A Rage for Order*, Belfast, 1992, p. 95)

July 1972, in which ninety-two people died, was the worst month of the troubles. But the level of violence fell sharply after that. Operation Motorman robbed the Provisionals of safe places where they could easily assemble bombs and snipe at soldiers.

LOYALIST VIOLENCE

Loyalist violence also rose in response to the IRA bombing campaign and to rumours that Whitelaw had talked to the Provisionals. Sectarian killing remained their favourite weapon and the RUC classified 121 of the 467 death in 1972 as 'sectarian'. They also petrol bombed Catholic homes and rioted with the police and army. In December they set off bombs in Dublin, killing two and in Cavan where two more died.

> **Sectarian killing:** The RUC used the word 'sectarian' to describe a Loyalist murder of a Catholic simply because of the victim's religion. Provisionals claimed they did not to kill people for sectarian reasons. But in reality they did though less often and less blatantly than the Protestant paramilitaries.

THE NORTHERN CONFLICT AFFECTS THE REPUBLIC

The rising violence in the North had an impact in the Republic. Up to 1972 there had been some sympathy for the IRA. Most people knew little about Northern Ireland but they had plenty of prejudices.

- They believed that all the people living in Ireland were one nation and should not be divided.
- They saw partition as a British plot to keep a foothold on the island and the IRA as continuing the unfinished business of the War of Independence up to 1921.
- They ignored the existence of the unionists. They did not try to understand their sense of British identity or why they feared Catholic rule and wanted to remain part of the United Kingdom.
- They heard of the discrimination against northern Catholics and wanted to help.
- Developments like the Civil Rights campaign, internment and Bloody Sunday strengthened these prejudices and contributed to sympathy for the IRA and its campaign.

But by 1972 most Catholic grievances had been removed, yet the IRA's violence went on. It began to seem pointless. What was to be gained by killing more innocent men, women and children? Slowly public opinion in the South began to change.

Patriotism is the last refuge of a scoundrel—*Samuel Johnson*

Many people found it hard to understand how 'loyalists' could claim to be loyal to Britain and its Queen while attacking British institutions

- Regular reporting by newspapers, radio and TV made people in the republic better informed about Northern Ireland.
- They began to understand that it existed because a million Protestants wanted to preserve their way of life and their British identity. They could never be bombed into a united Ireland.
- They also realised that, far from plotting to stay in Northern Ireland, the British would love to leave but stayed out of a sense of obligation to the unionists.
- And as violence increased in the North, the idea of a united Ireland became less and less appealing.

SOCIAL CHANGES IN THE SOUTH

Southerners also began to examine the things Protestants criticised about the republic, like the role of the Catholic Church and the ban on contraception and divorce. This led to a debate:
- Should these things be changed?
- And if so, should it be because they were obstacles to unity or because they were bad in themselves?

In 1972 in a referendum a large majority voted to remove the part of the Constitution which gave a 'special status' to the Roman Catholic Church. Later the law against contraception was eased. A referendum to remove the ban on divorce in the Constitution failed in 1986 but a second one succeeded in 1995.

ACTING AGAINST REPUBLICANS

Influenced by the changing views of their voters, southern governments began to take a tougher line against the IRA.

- In 1972 they closed down the Sinn Féin offices in Dublin and forbade RTÉ to broadcast interviews with IRA leaders.
- Irish army and Gardaí patrols were stepped up along the border, though it was far too long and winding to be sealed completely. Republicans and Loyalists could still move back and forth across it, evading the security forces on both sides.
- They strengthened the **Offences against the State Act** which since 1939 had been used to control 'subversives' (i.e. IRA members). Under this act they set up the '**Special Criminal Court**' in which three judges, acting without a jury, tried people accused of 'subversive activity'.

SEEKING A SETTLEMENT

1972 was the worst year of the troubles, with 467 people dead. But paradoxically that made it easier for Whitelaw to seek a peace settlement.
- The level of violence made moderates on both sides more eager for peace.
- The Irish government was more willing to discuss a new constitutional arrangement **within** Northern Ireland rather than demanding reunification.
- Also among republicans the Official IRA was on ceasefire while Operation Motorman had reduced the ability of the Provisionals to do harm.

The way seemed open for an agreement among constitutional politicians which, Whitelaw hoped, would outmanoeuvre the terrorists, end direct rule, restore devolved government to Northern Ireland and ensure peace and stability for the future.

QUESTIONS

1 Explain the difference between 'devolved government' and 'direct rule' in Northern Ireland.

2 Who was the first Secretary of State for Northern Ireland and what did he hope to achieve?

3 1972 was the worst year of violence in Northern Ireland. Select three violent episodes (other than Bloody Sunday) and write a paragraph about each of them.

4 What was 'Operation Motorman'? Was it a success?

5 Give three ways in which the troubles in Northern Ireland affected the republic and write briefly about each of them.

10 The Failure of the Sunningdale Agreement (Case Study)

OCTOBER 1972: THE FUTURE OF NORTHERN IRELAND

Throughout 1972 Whitelaw held meetings with all the parties, looking for a way to re-establish a devolved government in Northern Ireland. In October he produced a discussion document called *The Future of Northern Ireland* which included the ideas of power-sharing and a Council of Ireland.

MARCH 1973: THE BORDER POLL

By 1973 Whitelaw was ready to put his proposals into action. The first priority was to reassure the unionists that the Union with Britain was safe. To achieve this a referendum on the border – popularly known as the Border Poll – was held on 8 March. Nationalists, who were still engaged in a rent and rate strike over internment, boycotted it but unionists turned out in great numbers. Of the people on the voting register, 57 per cent voted and of those, 99 per cent supported Northern Ireland remaining part of the United Kingdom.

THE WHITE PAPER

White Paper: When a government wants to consult about an issue it produces a 'white paper' saying what it intends to do. This allows people to comment and suggest changes.

A few days after the Border poll Whitelaw produced a **White Paper** called *Northern Ireland Constitutional Proposals*.

- ◎ It guaranteed that Northern Ireland would remain part of the United Kingdom as long as the majority wanted that.
- ◎ It proposed an **Assembly**, elected by PR.
- ◎ The Assembly would set up a **Northern Ireland Executive** (government). But unlike the old government, the new Executive could '*no longer be solely based upon any single party, if that party draws its support and its elected representation virtually entirely from only one section of a divided community*'. This endorsed the idea of power-sharing.

  To mark the move away from the old Stormont, the British replaced the word 'parliament' with 'Assembly' and 'government' with 'Executive'.

- ◎ Once the parties had agreed to share power, the London government would transfer control over health, education, local government and some other matters to the Executive while keeping control over police, the legal system and other difficult matters. These might be transferred later if the Executive was successful.
- ◎ Finally, to acknowledge the nationalists' sense of Irish identity, the White Paper promised a Council of Ireland '*for consultation and co-operation between Northern Ireland and the Republic of Ireland*'.

Responses to the White Paper varied.

- The SDLP, which now represented moderate nationalists, welcomed power-sharing and a Council of Ireland as significant gains for the Catholic community. But republicans rejected it as reinforcing partition.

- Among unionists, Faulkner and the moderates gave it a cautious welcome. On 27 March, the Ulster Unionist Council accepted it by 381 votes to 231.

- But Paisley, Craig and the Orange Order condemned it completely. They would accept neither power-sharing nor any link with the republic. After the Ulster Unionist Council vote, Craig left the Unionist Party and set up his own Vanguard Party.

28 JUNE 1973: THE ASSEMBLY ELECTION

Elections to the new Assembly were held on 28 June. Republicans urged nationalists not to vote but the SDLP went into the campaign united in support of the White Paper proposals. This was also true of the two cross-community parties, the Northern Ireland Labour Party (NILP) and Alliance.

Among unionists, Paisley's DUP and Craig's Vanguard were equally united in their opposition to the proposals. Faulkner was in a more difficult position. Members of the Ulster Unionist Party were divided. Some supported power-sharing and others opposed it. He tried to ensure unity by insisting that all official Unionist candidates sign a pledge to support the White Paper. But each local Unionist branch picked its own candidates and some of them refused to take the pledge. As a result, there were both 'pledged' Unionist (i.e. supporters of Faulkner's line) and 'unpledged' Unionists led by Harry West, standing for election.

Faulkner also tried to reassure uneasy unionist voters by issuing a carefully worded manifesto. It stated that *'we are not prepared to participate in government with those whose primary objective is to break the Union with Great Britain'*. Some unionists thought this meant he would not share power with the SDLP but as he pointed out later, their **'primary** objective'** was power-sharing, not breaking the Union.

Selection of election posters, Assembly Elections, June 1973

The results of the 1973 Assembly election								
Party	SDLP	Alliance	NILP	Unionist Party (pledged)	Unionist Party (unpledged)	DUP	Vanguard	Loyalists
No. of seats	19	8	1	24	8	8	7	3
% of vote	22.10%	9.20%	2.50%	29.30%	10.50%	10.80%	11.40%	4.20%

In favour of power-sharing   *Against power-sharing*

THE RESULTS OF THE ELECTION

The results (Table A) were disappointing for Whitelaw and showed how deep the divisions in Northern Irish society were.

- The lack of enthusiasm for the White Paper proposals among unionists was very clear. Faulkner's section of the UUP won only twenty-four seats and 211,000 first preference votes, while the combined anti-White Paper unionists won twenty-six seats and 230,000 first preferences. Faulkner's weakness became even clearer when two of his 'pledged' candidates said they could not support a deal with the SDLP.
- Nationalists were also divided but this was not so obvious because Sinn Féin had not put up candidates for election. For the moment, the SDLP appeared as the sole voice of northern nationalism.
- The two 'cross-community' parties, Alliance and NILP won only nine seats between them.

PRELIMINARY DISCUSSIONS

When the Assembly met in July the bitterness between the sides erupted into rowdy scenes. DUP and Vanguard members engaged in obstructive tactics, name-calling, sit-ins and even physical attacks on unionist opponents. Despite this, however, there was a clear majority within the Assembly in favour of a negotiated settlement.

Preliminary discussions through the summer established that there were two key stages to the negotiations:

- getting parties from both sides to agree to set up a power-sharing Executive to rule Northern Ireland and

- getting agreement between the Executive and the British and Irish governments on a Council of Ireland and the role it should play.

It was agreed to deal with these two issues separately and once agreement was reached on both to launch them together.

AGREEING ON THE EXECUTIVE

The talks to set up an Executive began in Stormont on 5 October. There were six Unionist representatives led by Faulkner, six from the SDLP led by Fitt and three from Alliance led by Oliver Napier. The meeting was chaired by William Whitelaw with great skill and patience.

- The parties found it easy to agree in principle to set up an Executive. A much bigger problem was to decide how the ministerial positions were to be divided among the parties. Faulkner insisted that Unionists must have a majority if the Executive was to be trusted by the Protestant community. This issue almost led to a breakdown but it was finally agreed that there would be eleven Cabinet ministers – six Unionists, four SDLP and one Alliance.
- The idea of a Council of Ireland was also accepted. Faulkner wanted a Council composed of representatives of the Northern and Southern governments to deal with issues like tourism. But Hume in particular wanted it to contain representatives of the Dáil and the Assembly and to have wider powers, including control of policing. Whitelaw backed the SDLP, hoping that success would enable them to outmanoeuvre the IRA. Faulkner reluctantly accepted this because, as he wrote later, '*I was aiming for the supreme prize of co-operation*

against terrorism and to achieve it I was prepared to go along with a limited amount of nonsense from the nationalists' (Brian Faulkner, *Memoirs of a Statesman*, London, 1978, p. 218).

◉ For their part, the SDLP agreed to end the rent and rate strike against internment.

This phase of the talks ended on 21 November but because the SDLP insisted that 'nothing is agreed until everything is agreed' the Executive could not be set up until the second phase was completed.

WHITELAW REPLACED

The second phase of the negotiations was to decide on the structure and role of the Council of Ireland. It was to begin on 6 December at a civil service training college in Sunningdale in Berkshire, England.

Only days before it began, the Prime Minister, Edward Heath moved Whitelaw back to Britain to deal with trade unions who were causing problems for his government. This robbed the conference of his negotiating skill and the knowledge of Northern Ireland he had built up over the previous two years. His replacement, **Francis Pym**, had no experience of the intricacies of the northern situation and contributed little to the talks.

THE IRISH DELEGATION AT SUNNINGDALE

The Irish government delegation to the conference was led by the Taoiseach **Liam Cosgrave**. He had come to power in February as leader of a Coalition of Fine Gael and Labour, formed after Jack Lynch lost the general election. Among the other Irish delegates were the Foreign Minister, **Garret FitzGerald** of Fine Gael and **Conor Cruise O'Brien** of Labour.

When the Coalition first came to power, they saw the Council of Ireland as a token body, with representatives from North and South dealing with uncontroversial cross-border issues like tourism or transport. But John Hume convinced them that the Council should have real power so as

to pave the way to a united Ireland. He argued that the unionists were weak and divided and would therefore have to agree.

6–9 DECEMBER 1973: NEGOTIATING AT SUNNINGDALE

Heath chaired all the meetings during the conference. He was impatient with the unionists and admired John Hume. He therefore supported the nationalist desire to expand the powers of the Council of Ireland. This was agreed in principle but the delegates decided that the exact details would be settled later. The SDLP's Paddy Devlin and Conor Cruise O'Brien warned that it was not helpful to squeeze too much out of the unionists but their advice was ignored.

Faulkner and the British had hoped that the Irish government would agree to do certain things in return for a Council of Ireland but they were disappointed.

◉ They wanted the Irish government to guarantee that they would **extradite** IRA members, arrested in the republic, to Northern Ireland for trial. But the Irish negotiators pointed out that they could not promise this. The extradition of suspects was the job of the courts and no democratic government could tell judges what to do.

> **Extradite:** Send a person wanted for a criminal offence in another country back to that country for trial.

◉ Faulkner also wanted the Irish government to remove **Articles 2** and **3** of the Irish Constitution. Unionists found these articles offensive because they claimed that the South was entitled to rule the whole of the island. But the Irish ministers pointed out that only a referendum could change the Constitution. If one was held, it was likely that Fianna Fáil would oppose any change and it would be defeated. That would be worse than doing nothing at all. In any case, they claimed, the Articles were purely symbolic and had no practical effect.

Delegates from the British and Irish governments and the Northern Executive meeting in Sunningdale in December 1973

○ In the end all the Irish government felt able to give Faulkner was a verbal commitment to more co-operation on policing and a statement that they recognised the right of Northern Ireland to remain part of the United Kingdom as long as the majority there wanted it.

The Conference ended on 9 December.

1 JANUARY 1974: THE EXECUTIVE TAKES POWER

This agreement opened the way for the establishment of the power-sharing Executive in Belfast. It took over on 1 January 1974, with Brian Faulkner as Chief Minister and Gerry Fitt as his Deputy. But even as ministers settled into their offices and met their civil servants, the opponents of the agreement were gathering their forces.

ORGANISING UNIONIST OPPOSITION

While the talks were going on in Sunningdale, unionists who opposed an agreement had begun to unite. On 6 December the Orange Order, Vanguard, the DUP and dissident members of the Unionist Party like Harry West formed the **United Ulster Unionist Council** (**UUUC**) to resist power-sharing and a Council of Ireland.

Once the Sunningdale Agreement was announced, the Ulster Unionist Council, the governing body of Faulkner's party called a meeting for 4 January. A motion opposing the Council of Ireland was passed by 427 votes to 374. Brian Faulkner resigned as leader of the UUP and was replaced by Harry West.

Faulkner then set up the **Unionist Party of Northern Ireland** with his remaining pro-Agreement followers. He still had supporters within the unionist community and might have been able to increase their numbers if he had been able to show something in return for the concessions he had made. But the Agreement did not bring peace because the IRA and Loyalist paramilitaries continued their killing and developments in Dublin and London fatally undermined his position.

PROBLEMS IN THE REPUBLIC

In Dublin, Kevin Boland, a former Fianna Fáil minister who had resigned in 1970 in support of Haughey, took a case to the Supreme Court claiming that the Sunningdale Agreement was against the Constitution since it recognised Northern Ireland. The case lasted until March and damaged Faulkner in two ways:

○ To oppose Boland, the Irish government's lawyers had to make a strong case for Articles 2 and 3. This undermined the claim that they were merely symbolic and without real substance.

○ While the case lasted Cosgrave could not issue the statement that he had promised, recognising that Northern Ireland would remain part of the United Kingdom as long as the majority wanted it. When he was finally able to do so on 13 March, it was too late.

THE BRITISH GENERAL ELECTION

The worst blow Faulkner suffered came from Edward Heath. During 1973 there was a great deal of industrial unrest in Britain. To overcome it, Heath called a sudden general election for 28 February. He ignored pleas from Pym, Fitt and Faulkner that it would be disastrous for the Executive and the Agreement.

The United Ulster Unionist Council (UUUC) decided to treat the election as a kind of referendum on Sunningdale. Using the catchy slogan, *'Dublin is only a Sunningdale away'*, they put up one anti-Agreement candidate in each of the North's 12 Westminster constituencies. Faulkner's new party was not yet properly organised but it put up candidates who competed for votes with the other power-sharing parties, Alliance, SDLP and NILP.

In the eyes of many unionists the result of the election robbed Faulkner of any legitimate claim to govern Northern Ireland. Over 366,000 unionists (51 per cent of the total electorate) voted for UUUC candidates compared with 94,000 (13 per cent) who supported Faulkner's party. Paisley, Craig and West were all elected and the UUUC won eleven of the twelve Westminster seats. Only Gerry Fitt won a seat on the pro-Agreement side.

LABOUR RETURNS TO POWER

In Britain, Heath was defeated and Harold Wilson returned as Prime Minister. He appointed **Merlyn Rees** to be Northern Secretary. Rees was familiar with Northern Ireland, having been the Labour spokesman on it for several years. But he was an indecisive man, inclined to hesitate and question

Merlyn Rees who became Secretary of State for Northern Ireland after Labour won the British general election

Courtesy: Getty

before acting. The new government promised to support the Sunningdale Agreement but they were not as committed to it as the Conservatives, who had created it.

THE ULSTER WORKERS' COUNCIL (UWC)

None of these developments could destroy the Executive, though they did undermine its credibility. Ministers continued to administer their departments and on the whole they worked well together. The Assembly remained, though its meetings were discredited by the violent and abusive behaviour of some of the Anti-Agreement members. It was the decision of a small group of unionist workers which finally overthrew the power-sharing Executive.

Discrimination in employment over the years meant that in some important Northern Ireland industries the workforce was almost entirely Protestant. The **Ulster Workers' Council** (UWC) was a group of loyalist workers in some of these industries – shipbuilding, engineering and above

'Sure we're loyal to the Crown — when's our coronation?'

Did the cartoonist support or oppose the Worker's Council? Support your answer by referring to the cartoon

all, electricity generation. They had suggested a strike to some anti-Agreement politicians but were ignored. On 15 May, after the Assembly passed a vote of confidence in the Executive, they acted by themselves and called a strike.

MAY 1974: THE UWC STRIKE

Loyalist paramilitaries then became involved. Their 'tartan gangs' began to 'persuade' workers not to report for work. If that failed, they sent men into factories to 'suggest' that they close. They blocked roads with makeshift barricades of burnt-out cars and busses where youths armed with wooden clubs turned back lorries delivering milk, groceries or petrol. So many buses were hijacked that the service was cancelled.

But the strikers' main weapon was their control of the power stations. Within days they had cut electricity output by 60 per cent. That forced the closure of more factories, left people without lights or cookers, endangered sewerage plants and threatened the lives of people in hospitals.

The British army and the RUC stood by while all this went on. A few attempts were made to dismantle barricades but in general soldiers and police did not touch them. In places they were seen chatting amicably with the strikers.

It quickly became clear that many Protestants supported the strike. Robert Fisk, an experienced journalist, reported a middle-aged woman saying:

> '*I know there has been intimidation and looting... But we are sick of Faulkner and his men and the Council of Ireland. We do not want to strike but the British must let us have a fair government not Sunningdale. We have stuck the bombing and the IRA and the British government's mistakes for five years, so we can certainly stick this strike for two or three weeks...*' (*The Times*, 22 May 1974)

Prosperous unionist farmers from Co. Down using their tractors to blockade Stormont at the end of the strike. This shows that support for the strike spread far outside the working class ghettoes

Courtesy: British Cartoon Archive

Courtesy: Getty

'Some dove! Why, it couldn't even stand up to hatching!'

Courtesy: British Cartoon Archive

1 What organisation, apart from the UWC, does this man belong to? Pick out three things in the cartoon that support your answer.
2 What has he done?
3 Do you think that is a fair assessment of his role in 1974? Explain your answer

The UWC also made sure they did not alienate their own people. They arranged for some supplies to get through, for grocers, bakers and chemists to open for a few hours a day and for social welfare payments to reach pensioners.

17 MAY: BOMBS IN DUBLIN AND MONAGHAN

On the 17 May two car bombs went off without warning in crowded Dublin streets and a third in the border town of Monaghan. Together they killed 32 people and injured many more. It was the highest casualty total for any one day throughout the thirty years of the troubles. Although no one was ever charged, loyalists were strongly suspected of carrying out the bombing. On hearing the news, one strike leader commented: *'there is war in the Free State and now we are laughing at them'*.

'Phew! Oi'm beginning to go off the idea of a united Ireland meself.'

Courtesy: British Cartoon Archive

Explain the point the cartoonist is making here

THE GOVERNMENT RESPONSE

Meanwhile in Stormont, the Executive was increasingly isolated. They did not control the police or the army and they noted bitterly that Rees failed to use them to stop the strike. He replied that any attempt to occupy the power stations might have led to sabotage and that the army could not take on a large section of the Protestant population.

On 25 May Harold Wilson decided to broadcast to the nation but only made things worse when he said:

> *'… British taxpayers have seen the taxes they have poured out, almost without regard to cost – over £300 million a year this year …. They see property destroyed by evil violence and are asked to pick up the bill for rebuilding it. Yet people who benefit from all this now viciously defy Westminster, purporting to act as though they were an elected government; people who spend their lives sponging on Westminster and British democracy and then systematically assault democratic methods. Who do these people think they are?'*

This crass speech offended everyone including the nationalists and united the unionists against him. Over the next few days some took to wearing small pieces of sponge in their lapels as a gesture of defiance.

Faulkner tried desperately to buy off the opposition by getting the SDLP and the Dublin government to

The wreck of a car hit by an explosion in Talbot Street in Dublin. Three car bombs in Dublin and Monaghan killed 28 and injured 150. Four people died later in hospital

reduce the powers of the Council of Ireland. They agreed to postpone its implementation for several years but by then it was too late. An attempt to use the army to ensure petrol supplies failed when the strikers got to hear about it and reduced electricity supplies still further. Faced with hospital closures and sewerage overflows, the Executive resigned. The Sunningdale experiment in power-sharing had ended in failure.

WHY DID THE SUNNINGDALE AGREEMENT FAIL?

A bitter debate followed about the reasons for the failure.

- Nationalists blamed Merlyn Rees's unwillingness to use the police and army to stop the strike. It is possible that a quick response might have stopped it but Rees hesitated and once the strike was well established it is unlikely that army action would have worked.

- Some nationalists also suspected that the British army was opposed to the power-sharing Executive and keen to see it fail. There is no evidence that this was so but senior officers made it clear that they did not want to take on loyalists at the same time as they were fighting the IRA.

- The Labour government in London was also not very enthusiastic about the whole Sunningdale arrangement. This was partly because it was put in place by the Conservatives and partly because the election results made clear that only a minority of Protestants supported it.

WHY DID MANY UNIONISTS BACK THE UWC STRIKE?

It was the UWC strike that brought down the Executive. It succeeded partly through the ineptitude of the British government and partly because it clearly had the backing of a large proportion of the unionist community. Why was that?

- Some unionists supported the UWC action because they feared the Council of Ireland was intended to lead them into a united Ireland. These fears were reinforced by the Boland court case in the South and by speeches about Irish unity from some in the SDLP and some southern politicians.

- Others backed it because they deeply disliked power-sharing. They could not accept men like Gerry Fitt and Austin Currie, whom they blamed for the fall of Stormont, being part of their government.

1 What proposals about the future of Northern Ireland did Whitelaw put forward in 1972 and why did he organise a 'border poll' early in 1973?

2 What did the White Paper on Northern Ireland propose and how did the various parties respond to it?

3 What was the result of the Assembly elections in June 1973? Did the result strengthen or weaken the position of Brian Faulkner? Explain your answer.

4 Which parties were involved in the discussions that began on 5 October to set up an Executive and what had they agreed by 21 November?

5 Name and describe the various parties which took part in the final discussions in Sunningdale in December. What did they agree to?

6 What developments in (a) Northern Ireland (b) Britain and (c) the republic made things difficult for the Executive in its early weeks?

7 What groups formed the United Ulster Unionist Council (UUUC) and what policy did they adopt towards the Executive?

8 Who were the men who formed the Ulster Workers' Council? Describe the tactics they used against the Executive and explain why they were so successful.

9 How did the British government seek to deal with the UWC strike?

10 How do you account for the failure of the Sunningdale Agreement?

DOCUMENTS: A AND B

1: The Sunningdale Agreement
(extract from Northern Ireland Constitution Act, 1973)

A: An Act to make new provision for the government of Northern Ireland.
BE IT ENACTED by the Queen's most Excellent Majesty, by and with the advice and consent of the Lords Spiritual and Temporal, and Commons, in this present Parliament assembled, and by the authority of the same, as follows:–

Status of Northern Ireland

1. It is hereby declared that Northern Ireland remains part of Her Majesty's dominions and of the United Kingdom, and it is hereby affirmed that in no event will Northern Ireland or any part of it cease to be part of Her Majesty's dominions and of the United Kingdom without the consent of the majority of the people of Northern Ireland voting in a poll held for the purposes of this section ...

Devolution

2. (1) If it appears to the Secretary of State...

   (b) that a Northern Ireland Executive can be formed which, having regard to the support it commands in the Assembly and to the electorate on which that support is based, is likely to be widely accepted throughout the community, and that having regard to those matters there is a reasonable basis for the establishment in Northern Ireland of government by consent, he shall lay before Parliament the draft of an Order in Council appointing a day for the commencement of [an Executive].

> Try to include words or phrases from the documents in your answers.

B: Despite the chaos and loss of life that could result from a complete shut down of industrial power in the north, the Ulster Workers Council is resolved to carry on with its strike "until we get political change in our direction" .... The UWC'S case, in its own eyes, is a simple one. In February, Loyalist politicians won 11 of the 12 seats in the Westminster elections, roundly defeating candidates from all three pro-Executive parties. Despite this, however, and despite a border poll indicating (to them) no desire on the part of the electorate for association with the Republic, the Sunningdale Agreement is being pushed forward with all possible speed and a United Ireland seems just around the corner. (from: *Irish Times*, 20 May 1974)

QUESTIONS ON THE DOCUMENTS

Comprehension

1 What is Document A. Explain why it is important?

2 What does Document A say about (1) the status of Northern Ireland and (2) Devolution?

3 What, according to Document B, was 'the UWC's own case'?

Comparison

4 Do you think the members of the UWC quoted in Document B were aware of Document A and its contents? Explain your answer by referring to what they said.

Criticism

4 What light does Document B throw on the beliefs of the UWC strikers?

Contextualisation

5 What events led from the start of direct rule to the establishment of the Northern Ireland Executive in January 1974?

DOCUMENTS: C, D, E AND F

2: Why did the Sunningdale Agreement fail?

C: The sight of heavily subsidised and expensive farm machinery, bought largely out of public funds being used to block roads was hard to stomach... These were not the poor looking for a break or the unskilled worker who feared for his job or the unlettered fearful for his heritage. These were the rich, comfortable farmers of Co. Down, the backbone of conservative unionism who were concerned to retain the power and privilege they had enjoyed for generations. Their final act of demonstration was a cavalcade of farm machinery, led by muck spreaders loaded with ripe manure, to lay siege to the main buildings at Stormont... (See photo on p. 79) (from: Maurice Hayes, *Minority Verdict: Experiences of a Catholic Civil Servant*, Belfast, 1995, p. 199). *Note: Hayes was a senior civil servant who was in Stormont during the months of the Executive.*

> Try to include words or phrases from the documents in your answers.

D: The Executive was not brought down by the strikers alone. The majority of Protestants simply did not want the Executive and were passive supporters of the strikers. Glen Barr, a moving spirit, said later that he was surprised at the ease with which the Executive had fallen.... (from Basil McIvor, *Hope Deferred, experiences of an Irish Unionist*, Belfast, 1998, p. 121).
Note: McIvor was a moderate unionist, a supporter of Faulkner and member of the executive.

E: It became clear to me that that [Rees] was being swayed by a number of factors. First of all the evidence from the Westminster election of lack of popular support for the Faulkner Unionists... Second, army advice was almost certainly against any form of action that would bring the security forces into conflict with the majority Protestant community and bring close the nightmare of a 'war on two fronts'. Third, with all its unpleasant manifestations, the event was nevertheless a form of strike and a Labour government did not take readily to strike breaking... (from Ken Bloomfield, *Stormont in Crisis*, Belfast, 1994, p. 215). *Note: Bloomfield was a senior civil servant who worked closely with Faulkner during the life of the Executive.*

F:

The Ulster Nightmare

AS ILLINGWORTH SEES IT

This cartoon appeared in a British paper in June 1974

QUESTIONS ON THE DOCUMENTS

Comprehension

1   Who did the author of Document C see blockading Stormont? What conclusion did he draw from that?

2   What does the author of Document D believe brought down the Executive?

3   What, according to the author of Document E, were the factors that influenced Rees?

4   In the cartoon, who is the man in the jeep and what is the cartoon saying about his plight?

Comparison

5   What reason for the fall of the Executive, do Documents C, D and E all agree was very important?

6   What reason for the fall is given in the cartoon which is not mentioned in the other documents? How do you explain that difference?

Criticism

7   Which of the four sources here do you think is (a) the most reliable and (b) the least reliable for a historian studying the fall of the Northern Ireland Executive in 1974? Give reasons for your choice.

Contextualisation

8   Using the information from these documents and your own knowledge of Northern Ireland, do you consider that the Sunningdale experiment was doomed to failure?

Timeline for Case Study

1969: 29 April: Terence O'Neill resigns. Chichester Clarke becomes Prime Minister.

14 August: British troops in Northern Ireland.

1970: 21 August: The Social Democratic and Labour Party (SDLP) set up.

1971: 23 March: Brian Faulkner replaces Chichester Clarke.

9 August: Internment.

1972: 30 January: Bloody Sunday in Derry.

24 March: Stormont suspended; direct rule introduced. William Whitelaw becomes first Secretary of State for Northern Ireland.

21 July: Bloody Friday.

30 October: Discussion paper: *The Future of Northern Ireland* published.

1973: February: Fianna Fáil defeated in general election in the South; Coalition of Fine Gael and Labour led by Liam Cosgrave.

8 March: Border Poll.

20 March: White Paper: *Northern Ireland Constitutional Proposals* published.

27 March: Ulster Unionist Council votes to accept White Paper.

28 June: Elections to new Northern Ireland Assembly.

31 July: Assembly holds first meeting.

5 October: Talks to agree a power-sharing Executive begin.

21 November: Agreement reached on Executive.

4 December: Whitelaw replaced by Francis Pym.

6 December: Talks begin in Sunningdale. Opponents of the Executive set up the United Ulster Unionist Council (UUUC).

9 December: Agreement reached on Council of Ireland.

1974: 1 January: Executive takes office.

4 January: Ulster Unionist Council rejects Council of Ireland. Faulkner resigns and sets up Unionist Party of Northern Ireland.

28 February: General election in UK. Heath defeated. Wilson Prime Minister and Merlyn Rees is Northern Ireland Secretary. Opponents of Agreement win (UUUC) 11 of 12 Westminster seats.

14–28 May: Ulster Workers' Council strike. Executive collapses. Direct rule resumes.

THE LONG PATH TO PEACE
1974–1994

11 1974–1979: Stalemate

TRYING AGAIN: THE CONSTITUTIONAL CONVENTION

After the collapse of the power-sharing Executive, Rees made one last attempt to reach a compromise. In 1975 he held elections to the **Northern Ireland Constitutional Convention**. Its purpose was to consider what *'provision for the government of Northern Ireland is likely to command the most widespread acceptance throughout the community there'*.

But the elections only showed the strength of unionist opposition to power-sharing. Faulkner's UPNI won only 5 seats and 8 per cent of the vote against 47 seats and 55 per cent for the UUUC. This election marked the end of Brian Faulkner's career. In 1977 he was killed in a hunting accident. The SDLP took part in the election, winning 17 seats but they boycotted the Convention because it was not likely to agree to power-sharing.

When the Convention met, the victorious UUUC demanded a return to Unionist majority rule. Craig and a few others tried to make this more attractive to Catholics by suggesting to the SDLP that a future Unionist government might invite nationalists to take part in a 'voluntary coalition'. But Craig could not persuade a majority of Vanguard to support this idea. The party disintegrated and he was forced out of politics, leaving Ian Paisley as the main spokesman for hard-line unionism.

THE DOUBLE VETO LEADS TO STALEMATE

In 1976 the Convention produced a report demanding a return to majority rule. The British government rejected the report and closed it down. The failure of Sunningdale and the Convention to find a solution highlighted what came to be referred to as '**the double veto**'.

- Nationalists had shown their dislike of unionist majority rule and could prevent its restoration while:
- Unionists had shown they could stop nationalists getting what they wanted – power-sharing.

Harold Wilson examined other alternatives such as repartition with nationalist majority areas going to the South or even total British withdrawal. There were even secret talks with the Provisional IRA which led to a ceasefire through much of 1975. But in the end the British had to accept that there was a stalemate and that direct rule from London would have to continue for the foreseeable future.

THE PREVENTION OF TERRORISM ACT, 1974

Security was now their main preoccupation, especially after IRA bombs in Birmingham, Guildford and Woolwich in 1973–74 killed 28 people. In response the Westminster Parliament passed the **Prevention of Terrorism Act**. It allowed the police to question suspected terrorists for seven days before they were charged.

'ULSTERISATION'

The government also began a policy called '**Ulsterisation**'. This meant reducing the role of the British army while increasing the part played by the RUC and the Ulster Defence Regiment (UDR). Over the next few years, RUC numbers rose from 7,000 to 11,500 while the number of soldiers in Northern Ireland fell by half. The RUC got better weapons and, together with the 7,000 part-time soldiers of the UDR, took over much of the patrolling and searching. The army were now mainly used to control the border or to support the police in riot control.

The aim of Ulsterisation was to reduce British army casualties. The death of young soldiers had fuelled a 'troops out' demand in Britain that grew after the failure of power-sharing. An unforeseen side effect was to increase the bitterness between the two communities in Northern Ireland. The IRA, unable to reach soldiers, killed members of the RUC and the Ulster Defence Regiment (UDR). Almost all of them were Protestants who were easy targets because they lived locally. IRA sympathisers justified this as attacking 'legitimate targets' but to Protestants, and especially to the relatives and neighbours of the victims, these killings looked very like sectarian murder.

1976–79: ROY MASON

In September 1976 **Roy Mason** replaced Merlyn Rees as Northern Ireland Secretary. A tough former miner, he was determined to establish stability.

Almost immediately he had to face another political strike. Ian Paisley formed **the United Unionist Action Council** and threatened 'constitutional action' if the Convention report was not implemented. But Mason had learnt the lessons of 1974. When the strike began on May 2 1977 soldiers were drafted into the power stations and the RUC cleared barricades as soon as they were built. After

Roy Mason became Northern Ireland Secretary in September 1976. His previous position was as Minister for Defence and he got on better with the British army than Rees had

Courtesy: Getty

a few days the strike collapsed, partly due to these measures, and partly because the aim of restoring majority rule had less popular appeal than getting rid of power-sharing and the Council of Ireland.

MASON AND THE IRA

Mason also endeared himself to unionists by taking a stronger stand against the IRA than his predecessors. By 1977 he was claiming success.

- Anti-terrorist legislation allowed the police to hold and question suspects for several days at the Castlereagh Holding Centre in Belfast and at Gough Barracks in Armagh. This began to produce useful information about terrorist activities.
- There were rumours that some prisoners had been beaten to extract the information but the Diplock courts, where a single judge tried suspected terrorists, often convicted people on the basis of confessions made during questioning. As a result the number of terrorists in prison increased.
- Mason continued to free internees but insisted that from 1976 anyone imprisoned after a trial should be treated as an ordinary criminal.

- The level of violence fell and the death toll went from almost 467 in 1972 to around 100 a year in 1977 and 1978.

MASON'S ECONOMIC POLICY

Mason also hoped to undermine support for the violence by improving Northern Ireland's economy. It did badly in the 1970s.
- In 1974 the Belfast shipbuilders, Harland and Wolfe had to be taken into state ownership to stop them closing.
- Many multinational firms which had come to Northern Ireland in the 1950s and 1960s left, partly due to the violence, partly to the oil crisis of 1973 which pushed up prices.
- In the 1960s 30 per cent of workers were employed in manufacturing industries. This had fallen to 18 per cent by 1976.
- Unemployment averaged 10 per cent – twice as high as in Britain – but in some Catholic areas 50 per cent of the men were out of work.

Mason increased government spending in Northern Ireland at a time when it was being cut back in Britain. He protected Harland and Wolfe, increased the number of people employed by the government, and gave generous grants to community groups and local leisure centres.

*Years later a **DeLorean car** became famous when it featured in the Back to the Future films*

The most conspicuous example of state investment was the DeLorean project when the government gave millions to an American, John DeLorean, to set up a car company in West Belfast. After 8,000 sports cars were produced it collapsed when John DeLorean was charged with embezzling the funds.

THE UNIONISTS AFTER SUNNINGDALE

The UUUC, the alliance of unionist groups, that had defeated the Sunningdale Agreement fell apart after 1976. This was partly because of a disagreement about future policy.
- Many unionists wanted a return to majority rule in Stormont.
- Others believed that direct rule from London was the best way to protect their place within the United Kingdom.
- A few realised that the British would insist on power-sharing and talked about independence for Northern Ireland instead.

There was also a struggle for power between the Ulster Unionist Party (UUP) led by Harry West, Ian Paisley's Democratic Unionist Party (DUP) and William Craig's Vanguard. Vanguard soon disappeared, discredited by its close ties to the Loyalist paramilitaries and by Craig's support for a 'voluntary coalition' with nationalists during the Convention.

That left the UUP and the DUP to compete for leadership of the unionist community.
- The traditional party, the UUP suffered from poor organisation. West's weak leadership and divisions between those who wanted a return to Stormont and those who wanted direct rule to continue.
- By contrast, the DUP was united and well organised and had a charismatic leader in Ian Paisley. Despite his defeat in the second loyalist strike, the DUP expanded rapidly at the expense of the UUP in the late 1970s. Its share of the vote in local council elections rose from 4 per cent in 1973 to 26 per cent in 1981.

In 1979 the first direct elections for members of the **European Parliament** (MEPs) gave clear evidence

Courtesy: Alamy

James Callaghan. Harold Wilson unexpectedly retired in 1976 and James Callaghan became Prime Minister

James Molyneaux (1920–   ): A farmer from Co. Antrim, Molyneaux was active in Unionist politics and the Orange Order. Elected to Westminster in 1970, he opposed power-sharing and the Council of Ireland. When Faulkner resigned, he stood for the leadership but lost to Harry West.

of the DUP's success (Table A). Northern Ireland was treated as one constituency with the three MEPs to be elected by proportional representation.

Ian Paisley topped the poll with 29 per cent of the vote compared with 22 per cent for two UUP candidates, one of them Harry West. As a result, West lost the leadership to **James Molyneaux**.

MOLYNEAUX AS LEADER

A quiet man who believed that direct rule was the best option for unionists, Molyneaux concentrated on representing the unionist case in Westminster. This made political sense at that time.

Harold Wilson had resigned in 1976 and James Callaghan became Prime Minister. He needed UUP votes to stay in power and Molyneaux persuaded him to increase the number of Northern Ireland

MPs from twelve to seventeen. This and Roy Mason's tough attitude to the IRA, made more moderate unionists feel secure. Even after Callaghan lost the 1979 general election and Margaret Thatcher's Conservatives came to power with a large majority, they did not worry too much. They felt they could still count of the support of the British government because Thatcher claimed to be a strong supporter of the Union.

THE SDLP AFTER SUNNINGDALE

On the nationalist side, there was a similar power struggle between the SDLP and the IRA. As a result the SDLP became more nationalist and that led to the departure of the two socialist members, Paddy Devlin and the leader Gerry Fitt. They had always felt the party should be more socialist than nationalist and had hoped to appeal to working class unionists as well as to nationalists.

Table A

Elections to the European Parliament					
Party and candidate	DUP: Ian Paisley	SDLP: John Hume	UUP: John Taylor	UUP: Harry West	Alliance: Oliver Napier	Independent: Bernadette McAliskey
No. of votes	170,688	140,622	68,185	56,984	39,026	33,696
Percent	29.80%	25.50%	11.90%	10.00%	6.8%	5.9%

John Hume became leader when Fitt resigned in 1979. After the failure of Sunningdale he concluded that another purely internal Northern Ireland solution would fail. Wanting a united Ireland but also recognising the rights of unionists, he looked for a 'third way' which he called an 'agreed Ireland'. This would involve:

- Nationalists recognising that a united Ireland could only come with the consent of the unionists in Northern Ireland and
- the British saying that they would do nothing to stop a united Ireland if the unionists agreed to it.

This he thought would open the way to another power-sharing Executive.

After Hume was elected to the European Parliament in 1979 he used his position to make contacts in Europe and the United States as well as in Britain and the republic. His aim was to build a broad coalition of support for his ideas.

Gerry Adams (1948–   ) Gerry Adams was born into a Republican family in Belfast in 1948. He joined the IRA after the violence broke out in 1969 and soon emerged as a leader.

Courtesy: Corbis

GERRY ADAMS AND THE REORGANISATION OF THE PROVISIONAL IRA

The late 1970s also saw significant changes in the republican movement, including the emergence of new, northern-based leaders. The most notable of them was **Gerry Adams**.

Adams had been interned in 1971 but he was freed to take part in the talks with Whitelaw in 1972. Rearrested in 1973, he spent the next four years in the Maze prison where he had time to think about the future of the republican movement.

- He became critical of the older IRA leaders, who were mainly Dublin-based.
- He opposed the ceasefire they agreed to in 1975, arguing that it demoralised the IRA, led to internal feuds and encouraged it to engage in tit-for-tat sectarian killings with the Loyalist paramilitaries.
- He also came to believe that the British had no intention of leaving Northern Ireland. Therefore republicans must face up to a 'long war'. As part of this he felt they needed to

supplement the military campaign with political action.

After his release in 1977 Adams was involved in the reorganisation of the Provisionals. A new Northern Command was established, giving Adams and his ally, **Martin McGuinness**, more control over its activities. Big brigades were replaced by small Active Service Units, each set up to carry out a bombing, murder or robbery. With only a few members in each unit, they were less likely to be infiltrated by the security forces and if captured they would be unable to give away information about other units. He also encouraged the IRA's political wing, Sinn Féin to become more involved in political activity, after he was elected as its vice president in 1978.

THE PEACE PEOPLE

In the late 1970s the IRA was under pressure. Roy Mason's tough security policy took many of its active members out of circulation. Bombings and killings also caused a revulsion against violence in the working class communities from which the Provisionals drew much of their support. An early sign of this was the **Peace People**.

Courtesy: Getty

Mairead Corrigan leading a march of Catholic women across a 'peace line' into the Protestant Shankill Road in Belfast in 1976

On 10 August 1976 soldiers in Belfast shot dead the driver of an IRA getaway car which then ploughed into Anne Maguire and her four children, killing three of them and badly injuring the others. Maguire's sister **Mairead Corrigan** and **Betty Williams** then set up the Peace People to campaign against violence. Marches for peace drew large crowds of people from both communities in the North and the Republic. Corrigan and Williams were awarded in 1976 the Nobel Peace Prize but the movement fizzled out after quarrels about future policy.

A BI-PARTISAN APPROACH FROM WESTMINSTER

In 1979 the British Labour Party lost the general election and the Conservatives, led by Margaret Thatcher took power. But the change of government did not mark a change of policy. For years there had been an unspoken agreement between the two big political parties in Westminster that neither of them would criticise what the other was doing in Northern Ireland. This **bi-partisan approach** meant that a change of government in Britain did not mark a change of British policy in Northern Ireland. The new government would continue Labour's policy of trying to defeat the IRA and persuading the Northern Ireland parties to agree to share power.

QUESTIONS

1   What was the Constitutional Convention? What did the election to it say about public opinion in Northern Ireland? What did it demand in its report and how did the British respond to it?

2   Explain the concept of the 'double veto'. What was it likely to cause?

3   Write a paragraph on each of the following: The Prevention of Terrorism Act; Ulsterisation.

4   Who was Roy Mason? Explain his policy towards (a) the second loyalist strike, (b) republican violence and (c) Northern Ireland's economy.

5   How did the unionist parties fare after the defeat of the Sunningdale Agreement?

6   Describe how the SDLP developed after the failure of the power-sharing Executive.

7   Who was Gerry Adams and what part did he play in reorganising the IRA and Sinn Féin in the late 1970s?

8   Write a paragraph about the 'Peace People'.

9   Explain what is meant by a 'bi-partisan' policy towards Northern Ireland'.

⑫ The 1985 Anglo-Irish Agreement

THE H-BLOCKS AND THE 'DIRTY PROTEST'

It was the IRA hunger strikes that ended the stalemate which followed the collapse of Sunningdale. They were a protest against the government's decision to end the 'special category status' for terrorist prisoners. That had treated both republicans and loyalists very much like prisoners of war. They were:

- ⊙ housed in huts behind barbed wire,
- ⊙ allowed to wear their own clothes,
- ⊙ allowed to elect their own leaders and
- ⊙ allowed to refuse to do the work expected of ordinary criminals.

> The new prison at the Maze consisted of single-storey H-shaped blocks. This gave it its popular name of H-Blocks.

In 1976 Merlyn Rees replaced 'special category status' with a policy of '**criminalisation**'. Suspected terrorists were taken before the Diplock Courts and if found guilty were treated like common criminals. They were housed in a newly built prison in the Maze, had to wear prison clothes and obey prison rules.

From the start IRA prisoners protested that they were not criminals. At first they refused to wear prison clothes and were left in their cells with only a blanket for covering. When this failed to move the authorities, they refused to clean the cells, and then began to smear the walls with excrement. By 1978 there were over 300 prisoners involved in the 'dirty protest'. To support them, the IRA killed eighteen prison officers between 1976 and 1980.

HUNGER STRIKE

At first the 'dirty protest' did not attract much attention outside the prison system. In June 1979 Bernadette McAliskey (formerly Devlin) tried to change that by standing in the European election as a protest candidate on their behalf but only 5.9 per cent of voters supported her.

Finally in 1980 the prisoners themselves decided to go on hunger strike. Adams and other IRA leaders opposed this decision because a hunger strike was hard to maintain and failure would damage the republican movement. But the prisoners insisted and the first hunger strike began in October 1980. It ended after 53 days because they thought concessions were promised.

Murals painted on houses were used by both sides during the Northern conflict to get their message across and to mark out their territory

When nothing changed, the IRA leader in the Maze, **Bobby Sands**, began a second hunger strike on 1 March 1981. After two weeks another prisoner joined him, then a week later a third and so on. The aim was to have the maximum propaganda impact as, one by one, the men approached death.

An unplanned development increased the effect of the hunger strike. A few days after it began the Nationalist MP for Fermanagh-South Tyrone died suddenly. In the by-election that followed, republicans nominated Sands and persuaded the SDLP not to put up a candidate. In a straight fight with the UUP leader Harry West, Sands was elected by 30,492 votes to 29,046. The contest drew the world's media attention to Northern Ireland and put Bobby Sands and the hunger strike on news bulletins around the world.

1979–1990: PRIME MINISTER MARGARET THATCHER

The British Prime Minister confronting the hunger strikers was **Margaret Thatcher**. The first woman to lead a British party, she and the Conservatives won a huge majority in the 1979 election and through the 1980s they dominated the British political scene.

Shortly before the election Thatcher had experienced republican violence when a small republican group, the **Irish National Liberation Army**, had murdered her friend and advisor on Northern Ireland, Airey Neave. Soon after she became Prime Minister, the Provisionals had

Margaret Thatcher (1925–): Margaret Thatcher was born in 1925 and elected a Conservative MP in 1959. Edward Heath made her Education Minister. When he lost the 1974 election, she challenged him for the leadership and won.

Courtesy: Alamy

murdered the Queen's cousin, Lord Mountbatten and members of his family during their annual holiday in county Sligo and on the same day killed nineteen young soldiers in explosions at Warrenpoint in Co. Down.

MARGARET THATCHER AND THE HUNGER STRIKE

Thatcher was determined not to give in to the hunger strikers whom she saw simply as terrorists. When Sands died on 5 May 1981 she said in the

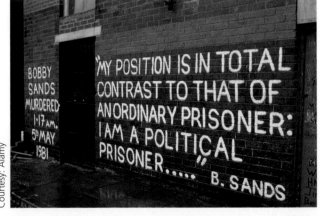

The way the hunger strikers divided opinion in Northern Ireland is clearly seen in these two photographs

Commons: '*Mr Sands was a convicted criminal. He chose to take his own life. It was a choice his organisation did not allow to many of its victims*'. She blocked any attempt at a compromise and let the hunger strikers die one by one.

Among nationalists the hunger strike aroused mixed emotions. Many, who hated the IRA's violence, also knew that most of these men were not common criminals. Reluctantly, they admired their courage and were angry when attempts at mediation by the Red Cross, the Vatican, the Irish government and many other groups and individuals failed. Over 100,000 people attended Sands's funeral. There were vicious riots in Belfast in which several people were killed by plastic bullets.

By August 1981 another ten hunger strikers were dead. There is evidence that the leaders of the IRA also discouraged compromise but nationalists blamed the deaths on Thatcher's intransigence. It was the prisoners' families who finally ended it. Helped by a prison chaplain, Father Denis Faul, they asked doctors to revive men who became unconscious. In October the remaining strikers called off their protest. They believed they had failed but many of their demands were quietly conceded by the new Northern Ireland Secretary, James Prior. Had this been done earlier some lives might have been saved and the IRA denied a propaganda victory.

THE IMPACT OF THE HUNGER STRIKES

The hunger strikes had a huge impact on events in Northern Ireland.

- The hunger strikes deepened the division between nationalists and unionists. Protestants saw the prisoners as criminals and their deaths as suicide. They could not understand why many Catholics, even those who abhorred the IRA and its activities, saw them as brave men willing to give up their lives for a cause, however misguided.
- Although at first republicans thought they had been defeated, the hunger strikes actually strengthened the IRA. New recruits joined them allowing them to continue their

A British soldier standing beneath an IRA mural

Courtesy: Alamy

campaign of bombing and destruction into the 1980s and 1990s.

- Sands' election victory showed republican leaders the value of political activity. With '*the ballot box in one hand and the Armalite in the other*' they revived Sinn Féin and began to contest local and national elections both in Northern Ireland and in the Republic. Several were elected to the Dáil and in 1983 Adams himself won the Westminster seat that Gerry Fitt had held since 1966, though he refused to take his seat in the Commons.
- The way Britain handled the hunger strikes damaged its reputation around the world. It also appalled the Irish government which knew it would strengthen republicans at the expense of moderate nationalists.

THATCHER'S POLICY TOWARDS NORTHERN IRELAND

With her stand against the hunger strikers, Margaret Thatcher reinforced her reputation as '*the Iron Lady*'. But her attitude to Northern Ireland was complex.

- She hated the IRA who had killed her friend Airey Neave and almost killed herself with a bomb in her hotel in Brighton during the 1984 Conservative Party conference. These and other incidents including the hunger strike, made her more determined than ever to defeat the 'terrorists'.

- As a British nationalist, she instinctively supported the Union between Britain and Northern Ireland. Her friend William Whitelaw convinced her that the best way to protect it was to set up a power-sharing government. As a result, she encouraged her Northern Ireland Secretaries, **Humphrey Atkins** and **James Prior** to continue looking for an agreement among the northern parties.
- Atkins published a White Paper and held talks on power-sharing in 1980 but failed to get agreement. In 1982 Prior came up with a plan for 'rolling devolution'. An Assembly was elected and he proposed handing power over to it bit by bit as the members reached agreement. This was the first election that Sinn Féin fought after the hunger strikes; they won 5 seats and 10 per cent of the vote. The SDLP boycotted the Assembly and it too failed to produce an acceptable government for Northern Ireland.

The lack of progress frustrated Thatcher and she was angered by the unionists' reluctance even to consider power-sharing. But although she would never consider abandoning Northern Ireland, she was a pragmatic politician. She knew that the conflict there damaged Britain's international reputation, drained its economic resources and killed its soldiers. She was therefore willing listen to those who also argued that an alternative way to peace might be found through collaboration with the Irish government.

There were several reasons for this:
- The main one was her belief that co-operation with the South might improve security. IRA men arrested in the South could be extradited to stand trial in Britain or the North, while cooperation along the border might make it more difficult for the IRA to move between North and South.
- Another was concern that Sinn Féin's election successes after the hunger strikes might destroy the SDLP, the voice of moderate nationalism. That would make power-sharing impossible.
- Pressure from the United States also influenced Thatcher who highly valued Britain's 'special relationship' with the US. From the mid-1970s Irish diplomats and John Hume worked hard to convince leading Irish Americans like **Senator Edward Kennedy** that they must oppose violent republicanism and give their support to moderates like John Hume and the SDLP. These men won the backing of **President Ronald Reagan** who in turn encouraged Margaret Thatcher to talk to the Dublin government.

TAKING A TOUGH LINE AGAINST THE IRA

In the South too, attitudes to Northern Ireland changed as the 1980s progressed. Although violence was mostly confined to the North, there had been enough incidents in the republic to raise fears that it could spill over. As a result all governments took a tough line against the IRA. A '**Special Criminal Court**' of three judges acting without a jury tried terrorist-related cases. It could imprison a person for membership of the IRA on no stronger evidence than the belief of a senior Garda.

Courtesy: Getty

The wrecked car in which Thatcher's adviser Airey Neave was killed by a bomb at the entrance to Westminster on 31 March 1979

QUESTIONING TRADITIONAL ATTITUDES TO PARTITION

Since 1920 most nationalists believed that the British had partitioned Ireland because they had strategic and economic interests there which they were unwilling to let go. The IRA campaign was based on this belief and its aim was to make it economically and politically unattractive for the British to remain in the North.

But after the failure of the Sunningdale experiment, the continuous violence and the hunger strikers, moderate nationalists were forced to ask painful questions about this traditional view of partition.

- If the million Protestants in Northern Ireland were so clearly opposed to something as moderate as power-sharing, what hope was there of getting them to accept a united Ireland if the British were to leave?
- Might a British departure be followed by a more vicious civil war – and one which would certainly involve the republic?
- Maybe nationalists should stop talking about a united Ireland and try instead to understand unionist fears and do something about them?
- Perhaps the Irish and British governments should co-operate in containing violence while working together to find some kind of alternative settlement?

GARRET FITZGERALD AND CHARLES HAUGHEY

One man who contributed significantly to this debate was **Garret FitzGerald**. As Foreign Minister in the 1973 Coalition, he was involved in negotiating the Sunningdale Agreement. He also encouraged Irish diplomats in London, Brussels and Washington to talk to leading politicians and encourage them to support moderate parties and moderate solutions. After the Coalition lost the 1977 election to Fianna Fáil, he was elected leader of Fine Gael. He had close ties to John Hume and the SDLP and was worried about the growth in support for Sinn Féin after the hunger strikes. If it continued he feared that Sinn Féin might destroy the SDLP and perhaps destabilise the republic.

FitzGerald's main rival, **Charles Haughey**, was more of a traditional nationalist. After being sacked by Jack Lynch in 1970 on the suspicion of running guns to the IRA, he rebuilt support within Fianna Fáil and in 1979 ousted Lynch as party leader and Taoiseach. This created deep divisions within Fianna Fáil, partly due to concern about Haughey's personal activities, partly due to his attitude to Northern Ireland. In the end some of Haughey's opponents left the party to form the **Progressive Democrats** (PDs), thus weakening Fianna Fáil.

In the early 1980s the republic experienced a period of unstable governments. In July 1981 Haughey lost an election to a Fine Gael/Labour Coalition led by FitzGerald. It fell in February 1982 and Haughey returned with a minority Fianna Fáil government, only to lose office again to FitzGerald in December. This Coalition survived to March 1987.

THATCHER AND HAUGHEY

Haughey was Taoiseach when Thatcher came to power in 1979 and they met for talks. At first they got on well but relations deteriorated when Haughey suggested in public that a united Ireland might be possible and later when he refused to support Britain's position in the war with Argentina over the Falkland Islands in 1982.

1983–84: THE NEW IRELAND FORUM

Garret FitzGerald returned as Taoiseach in December 1982. He felt that nationalists who opposed violence should try to work out their ideas about the future of Ireland and their attitude to Northern Ireland. To achieve this he set up the **New Ireland Forum** in 1983. Meetings were held in Dublin Castle and attended by all constitutional parties. Members listened to ideas and opinions from a broad range of people including Catholic bishops, Protestant clergymen and individual unionists, though no unionist party was willing to go to Dublin to give evidence. The discussions at the Forum helped to change southern attitudes to partition and the northern conflict.

The leaders of Constitution Nationalists at the New Ireland Forum. They were Dick Spring, leader of the Labour Party, Charles Haughey, leader of Fianna Fáil, Taoiseach Garret FitzGerald, leader of Fine Gael and John Hume, leader of the SDLP

Courtesy: Photocall Ireland

In 1984 the report of the Forum was published. To get Haughey's support, it was more nationalistic than FitzGerald had hoped. It listed nationalist aims in order of preference as:

- a single, all-Ireland state,
- a federal Ireland, with north and south having their own local governments and
- joint authority by Britain and the republic over Northern Ireland.

But when the report appeared Haughey rejected the second and third options, stating that only an all-Ireland state would do. Unionists denounced the whole lot. Thatcher, when asked about each option in turn, replied OUT! OUT! OUT! This was humiliating for FitzGerald and relations between Britain and the republic seemed worse than ever.

THE 1985 ANGLO-IRISH ('HILLSBOROUGH') AGREEMENT

Within a very short time the situation had changed completely. This was partly because for several years senior civil servants from London and Dublin had been meeting regularly to discuss common problems. This and the experience of working together in the European Union built up understanding and trust between individuals in the two governments.

However none of that would have mattered if Thatcher had not personally liked and trusted FitzGerald and hoped to get the republic's help with the security situation in Northern Ireland. At a meeting in London FitzGerald convinced her

that only a radical breakthrough by the two governments would end the alienation of northern Catholics and get them to support the security services.

This led to talks through most of 1985. They ended when the two leaders signed the **Anglo-Irish Agreement** at Hillsborough Co. Down on 15 November.

- The Agreement began by stating firmly that the status of Northern Ireland would only change with the consent of the majority of its people ('*the principle of consent*').
- It went on to declare that Northern Ireland would remain part of the United Kingdom but
- an **Inter-Governmental Conference**, jointly chaired by the Northern Ireland Secretary and

Courtesy: Martyn Turner

F.O.R.U.M. R.E.P.O.R.T....

1 Who is the man in the top image? What does he see in the chart?
2 Who is the woman in the bottom image? What does she see?
3 Explain the point the cartoonist is making. Do you agree or disagree with it? Explain your answer

Garret FitzGerald and Margaret Thatcher signing the Anglo-Irish Agreement in Hillsborough in 1985

Courtesy: Mirrorpix

the Irish Foreign Minister, would meet regularly. It would discuss security as well as issues that concerned the Catholic community such as discrimination, the teaching of Irish and the flying of flags and would make '*a determined effort*' to sort out differences.
- Civil servants from London and Dublin would be permanently based in **Maryfield**, near Belfast to support the Inter-Governmental Conference.

NATIONALIST REACTIONS TO THE AGREEMENT

- The IRA and Sinn Féin denounced the Agreement.
- So did Charles Haughey, saying it 'copper-fastened partition'. He later changed his attitude when it became clear that a majority of people in the republic and in Fianna Fáil supported the Agreement.
- There were some nationalists who felt it was unfair that the unionists had not been consulted about the Agreement. One was **Mary Robinson**, the future President, who resigned from the Irish Labour Party in protest.

UNIONIST REACTIONS TO THE AGREEMENT

For Unionists, the Agreement was a political nightmare because it placed officials and ministers from the South right at the heart of Northern Ireland's government. It took them completely by surprise. The UUP leader, James Molyneaux, had

refused to join in the talks because he believed his absence and Thatcher's support for the Union would protect them. As a result he had not been told about the progress of the negotiations and was quite unprepared for what happened.

RESISTING THE AGREEMENT

Feeling abandoned and betrayed, unionists of all parties united in protest.
- About 100,000 people turned out for a huge '*Ulster says no*' rally in central Belfast. Molyneaux shared the platform with Ian Paisley who said: '*Where do the terrorists return to for sanctuary? To the Irish Republic. And yet Mrs. Thatcher tells us that that republic must have some say in our Province. We say never, never, never, never.*'
- Similar large rallies took place at many venues around Northern Ireland and over 400,000 people signed a joint UUP/DUP petition against the Agreement.
- Loyalist workers called protest strikes which were marked by riots. Loyalist paramilitaries threatened to kill the civil servants and ministers involved in Maryfield. They also attacked RUC officers and intimidated about 500 out of their houses.
- Unionist councillors boycotted council sittings but went back after realising that this left their opponents in control.
- Fifteen unionist MPs resigned their Westminster seats and stood again in the by-elections as anti-Agreement candidates. Their aim was to stage a kind of referendum on the Agreement but other parties only stood against them where they thought they could win. They lost one of the seats to the SDLP.

Courtesy: Getty

Unionist resistance continued through 1986 but it proved futile.

- The violence of some protesters put off moderate unionists.
- The Inter-governmental Conference and the Maryfield Secretariat were designed to resist pressure and remained in place.
- Margaret Thatcher again lived up to her reputation and refused to bend.

THE RESULT OF THE AGREEMENT

Thatcher later questioned the value of the Agreement because it did not improve security or bring about the defeat of the IRA. But it did improve relations between Britain and the republic and helped to build understanding and trust between the two governments, which was the basis of the later peace process.

DUP WEAKENED AND THE UUP STRENGTHENED

In the years after the signing of the Anglo-Irish Agreement, the DUP was weakened and the UUP grew stronger. Many moderate unionists disliked the way DUP leaders like Paisley and Peter Robinson were seen in the company of loyalist paramilitaries. They also blamed the DUP whose opposition to even minor concessions to Catholics had, they felt, opened the way for this much bigger blow to unionism.

THE RUC AND LOYALIST PARADES

One result of the Agreement was a change in the RUC's attitude to Orange parades. This came about because the British wanted nationalists to accept the police but that would only happen if they appeared fair and even-handed in the way they enforced the law. The RUC accepted that some parades caused problems when they went through nationalist areas and rerouted them. Violence flared up between the Orangemen and the RUC in Portadown in 1985 and 1986 when loyalists claimed the right to march in areas where the majority of the residents were Catholic.

In 1987 the regulations governing parades were changed. Traditional Orange parades lost their privileged position and were put on the same level as all other parades. From now on they needed police approval before they could proceed. Orange leaders protested that the RUC had sold out to Dublin and that the rerouting of their parades amounted to an attack on their civil and religious liberties but their protests were largely ignored.

QUESTIONS

1 Explain the terms: 'special category status' and say how it began. What did the term 'criminalisation' mean? Explain why it was introduced.

2 Write a paragraph about the origin and progress of the hunger strikes. What impact did they have on Northern Ireland?

3 What was Margaret Thatcher's attitude to Northern Ireland?

4 How did southern attitudes towards Northern Ireland change between the start of the troubles and the Anglo-Irish Agreement? What part did Garret FitzGerald and Charles Haughey play in these changes?

5 What was the New Ireland Forum?

6 Give three reasons why Margaret Thatcher was willing to negotiate the Anglo-Irish Agreement in 1985. List the main points of the Agreement.

7 How did (a) nationalists and (b) unionists feel about the Anglo-Irish Agreement? What steps did the unionists take to destroy the treaty? Why did they fail?

8 What was impact of the Anglo-Irish Agreement? How did the Anglo-Irish Agreement affect the unionist parties?

(13) 1985-1994: From Agreement to Ceasefire

A NEW DEPARTURE IN SINN FÉIN POLICY

The Anglo-Irish Agreement and Thatcher's resistance to unionist pressure impressed some republicans like Gerry Adams and marked the start of a debate within republican ranks. If the British were prepared to stand up to unionists and make a deal with Dublin over their heads, perhaps political involvement might achieve what violence could not?

Gerry Adams was also influenced by Sinn Féin's success during the hunger strikes in winning Dáil and local council seats in the South. But he believed that the Sinn Féin policy of **abstention** from the Dáil damaged their chances there. In 1986 he and Martin McGuinness persuaded the Sinn Féin Árd Fheis to allow Sinn Féin TDs to take their seats in Dáil Éireann. The decision to end abstention angered older republicans who left to set up the '**Republican Sinn Féin**'.

Abstention: In 1918 Sinn Féin MPs refused to take their seats in Westminster. Later, after the 1921 Treaty, extreme republicans also abstained from Dáil Éireann, first because of the Oath to the King, later because it only represented the 26 counties, not the all-Ireland republic they claimed to want. Sinn Féin still abstains from Westminster.

Because of the political instability in the republic in the early 1980s, Adams hoped that after the next election Sinn Féin TDs might hold the balance of power in the Dáil. That did not happen. Once the impact of the hunger strikes wore off, Sinn Féin found that their ongoing campaign of killing, bombing and bank robberies did not appeal to the vast majority of southern voters. In the 1987 election, which returned Haughey to power in coalition with the PDs, they got less than 2 per cent of the vote and won no Dáil seats.

LIBYAN ARMS

In the North, support for the IRA's 'armed struggle' remained strong in republican areas. The level of violence actually increased after the Anglo-Irish Agreement. Part of the reason for this was the support the IRA got from the Libyan dictator **Colonel Gaddafi**, after he quarrelled with Britain in 1984. He sent them four shipments of arms including two tons of semtex explosives, armour-piercing machine guns and anti-aircraft guns that could bring down British army helicopters. British and Irish intelligence officers were quite unaware

Gerry Adams from Belfast and Martin McGuinness from Derry emerged as leading figures in Sinn Féin/IRA during the 1980s

Courtesy: Photocall Ireland

Courtesy: British Cartoon Archive

"OH, I DID LOVE GARRET WITH HIS CURLY HAIR AND WINNING WAYS – THEN HE LOST HIS JOB – LEFT ME ON MY OWN WITH BABY.."

In the 1987 election Charles Haughey replaced Garret FitzGerald as Taoiseach. In opposition he had opposed the Anglo-Irish Agreement. What point is this cartoon making about his attitude?

of this development until the French intercepted one of the arms ships in 1987.

Libyan arms allowed the IRA to mount a number of 'spectaculars' – large explosions in the centres of towns. Their declared aim was to inflict economic damage rather than kill people but casualties were inevitable. On 11 November 1987 the IRA disgusted even some of its own supporters when it set off a bomb at a **Remembrance Day** ceremony in Enniskillen, killing eleven Protestants. The courage and dignity of Gordon Wilson whose daughter died beside him in the blast won admiration around the world.

EXPANDING THE THREAT

The IRA always insisted that members of the RUC and UDR, prison officers and British soldiers were **'legitimate targets'** because it was fighting a war and they were part of the enemy's forces. But in 1986 they expanded their list of 'legitimate targets' to include civil servants, building contractors, caterers and others doing work for the security forces. This led to a number of brutal killings of ordinary people. Some were Catholic but most were Protestant which to most outsiders looked more like sectarian murders than the clean war the IRA claimed to be fighting.

A DIRTY WAR

The British fought back in a variety of ways:

- They drafted in the **SAS** to take on IRA active service units in border areas. This led to a number of episodes in which IRA volunteers were intercepted and killed. On 8 May 1987 eight IRA men were killed as they attacked an RUC barracks in **Loughgall**, Co. Armagh. Ballistic tests on the guns captured showed they had been used in 33 raids or murders. Republicans protested that the men need not have been killed and claimed there was a 'shoot to kill' policy but many people felt that the army actions were justified.

  > **SAS** = Special Air Service, the secretive counter-terrorism unit of the British army.

- Another tactic was the use of **'super-grasses'**. They were members of the IRA who informed on their comrades in return for immunity from prosecution, money and a chance to start a new life somewhere else. Super-grass information was at first accepted by the courts and led to the imprisonment of some republican activists. But suspicions grew about how reliable much of the super-grass evidence was. Courts became more sceptical and the system ended.

TIT-FOR-TAT KILLING

Loyalists also increased their violence in response to the 1985 Agreement. Younger, more ruthless men took over the UDA and between 1986 and 1989 they killed over 40 Catholics. They claimed to be targeting Sinn Féin and IRA activists but because they had difficulty identifying them, most of their victims were innocent Catholics, chosen at random. In the early 1990s they succeeded in killing a number of IRA men and Sinn Féin councillors. Republicans claimed that they were able to do so because the security forces were feeding them information.

THE GIBRALTAR KILLINGS AND THEIR AFTERMATH

In the almost constant violence some episodes stood out. One occurred in March 1988:

- In Gibraltar an undercover SAS unit shot dead three IRA activists, one of them a woman. The British at first claimed that they were shot to stop them bombing the British army base but it soon became clear that they were unarmed and did not have a bomb.
- A big crowd and the international press turned out for their funerals in Belfast. In the graveyard a loyalist, Michael Stone, fired shots and threw hand grenades into the mourners, killing three of them. The RUC then arrested Stone.
- One of his victims was an IRA activist. While he was being buried a few days later, a British army car containing two soldiers accidentally

drove by the funeral parade. Thinking this was another loyalist attack, the crowd turned on the soldiers and brutally beat them to death. This too was televised and shown around the world.

LIVING WITH FEAR

Episodes such as these increased the level of fear in Northern Ireland. Fear made it difficult to have a normal social life. Town centres were sealed off and people were searched when they entered shops or bars. Communities enclosed themselves behind increasingly elaborate 'peace walls' in an attempt to stop petrol bombers and rioters. The economy was also damaged since few foreign firms wanted to set up in Northern Ireland while the violence persisted. Unemployment remained high and only a very large British subsidy kept the economy from collapsing.

An IRA sign in South Armagh where several British soldiers were killed

Courtesy: Alamy

As this Derry mural shows, Michael Stone became a hero in some loyalist areas. For Republicans, the heroes of this episode were the 'Gibraltar Three'

Courtesy: Corbis

TENSIONS WITHIN SINN FÉIN

IRA violence also caused problems for the Sinn Féin Party. After the hunger strikes, Sinn Féin candidates became active in local politics, helping people with issues like housing, vandalism, drug-dealing and joy-riding.

> **Joy-riding:** stealing cars to race them in housing estates.

- Non-violent republicans were attracted by the Sinn Féin's social activity but were put off from voting for them by the continuing IRA violence.
- Bombing town centres and setting fire to shops and offices destroyed jobs. Some Sinn Féin councillors began to point out to the IRA the contradiction between this and their claim to be creating work and encouraging investment in their areas.
- Sinn Féin would not turn to the RUC to deal with vandals, drug dealers and joy-riders but got the IRA to impose 'punishment beatings' and 'kneecappings'. This brutal form of justice was popular in ghetto areas that the IRA controlled but made Sinn Féin unattractive to voters outside of them.

These contradictions helped a debate to begin within republicanism. What was the best way forward? Could they win the war? If not, might it not be better to ceasefire so that talks could begin?

'TALKS ABOUT TALKS'

This debate was further encouraged by secret talks between Gerry Adams and John Hume and between Adams and a representative of the Taoiseach Charles Haughey in 1988. Both made it clear to Adams that a '**pan-nationalist**' alliance to negotiate with the British was possible but only on the basis of an IRA ceasefire which Adams either could not or would not deliver at that time.

Meanwhile the British moved back to a more pro-unionist stance in the late 1980s. There were several reasons for this:

- The Anglo-Irish Agreement had not given them the security improvements they had hoped for.
- The re-election of Charles Haughey as Taoiseach in 1987. He had denounced the

From the early 1970s, the RUC had very little influence in Catholic ghetto areas in Belfast and Derry. The IRA controlled those areas and imposed violent punishments on those who broke its rules

Agreement and Thatcher suspected him of republican sympathies.

- Disagreements with the Irish government over the extradition of IRA suspects and the fate of the innocent men imprisoned for bombings in Guilford and Birmingham in the 1970s.
- A desire to end unionist isolation and the more flexible attitude to discussions shown by the UUP leader James Molyneaux.

In 1990 the Northern Secretary, **Peter Brooke**, launched a new series of inter-party talks. The UUP were involved as were the DUP after the British hinted that the Anglo-Irish Agreement might be temporarily suspended. The talking continued until 1992 and even involved a visit by Molyneaux to Dublin to meet the Taoiseach. But they collapsed through lack of agreement over the future of the Inter-Governmental conference and the Maryfield Secretariat, set up under the Agreement.

BRITISH OVERTURES TO THE IRA

The failure of these talks led the British to explore ways of encouraging the IRA to cease fire. Secret contacts had existed for years and the British almost certainly had informers within the Sinn Féin/IRA leadership. This kept them in touch with the ongoing republican debate about the future.

One thing that concerned Republicans was whether the British would leave Northern Ireland voluntarily if unionists and nationalists could agree on a united Ireland. Brooke made a number of comments which clearly signalled that they would. The most important was a speech in November 1990, in which he said that:

> '... the British government has no selfish strategic or economic interest in Northern Ireland .... Britain's purpose ... is not to occupy, oppress or exploit but to ensure democratic debate and free democratic choice'.

THE HUME-ADAMS TALKS

This backed up what John Hume had been telling Gerry Adams during their secret talks. Hume was trying to persuade Adams that the traditional republican view of partition was wrong. The British, he argued, only stayed in Northern Ireland because of a sense of obligation to the unionists. Therefore the 'problem' in Northern Ireland was not the British presence but one million unionists. A united Ireland depended on winning them over, not on forcing the British to withdraw.

Hume's argument was strengthened by the end of the Cold War in 1990. After that it was no longer possible to believe that Britain needed Northern Ireland as a military base or feared it would be occupied by the Soviet Union if they left.

After Brooke's speech Hume suggested that the SDLP, Sinn Féin and the Irish government seek a joint declaration on Irish unity from the British government. Based on Hume's idea of an 'Agreed Ireland' rather than a 'united Ireland', the declaration would have:

- The British acknowledging the Irish right to self-determination and
- Nationalists acknowledging that unity was impossible without the consent of the unionist majority in Northern Ireland.
- It also suggested that the British would agree to 'persuade' the unionists to agree to unity.

The republicans did not accept this proposal, seeing it as giving the unionists a veto on Irish unity, but Hume won the backing of the southern government.

REPUBLICAN BOMBS IN ENGLAND

The problem Adams faced was how to convince his hard-line followers that more could be achieved by talks than by continuous violence. For many of them, that would mean the years of struggle and suffering had been pointless. Perhaps to show them that the IRA would enter such talks from a position of strength, the IRA resumed its activity in England. In 1990 it assassinated a senior Conservative politician and in January 1992 fired mortars into the garden of 10 Downing St where the British cabinet was meeting. In 1992 a massive bomb in the financial centre of London caused £800 million worth of damage – almost as much as the cost of all the Irish violence to date.

PRESIDENT CLINTON

The election of Bill Clinton as President of the United States in 1991 helped to strengthen moderate voices within republicanism. Influenced by a group of wealthy and powerful Irish Americans, he took an interest in Irish issues even before becoming President. During the election campaign he had promised to appoint an American envoy to help establish peace and to give a visa to Gerry Adams to let him visit the USA. But clearly these concessions were also dependent on the promise of an IRA ceasefire.

ALBERT REYNOLDS AND JOHN MAJOR

In 1992 Charles Haughey was replaced as leader of Fianna Fáil and Taoiseach by **Albert Reynolds**. He was a pragmatic businessman who liked making deals and was not burdened with republican ideology. He had also become friends with the new British Prime Minister, **John Major**, when they worked together at EU meetings. Major, who replaced Thatcher as Prime Minister in 1990, was at first reluctant to consider a deal with nationalists but his personal friendship with Reynolds helped to change his mind.

Courtesy: Corbis

John Major, the British Prime Minister, and Taoiseach Albert Reynolds shaking hands after the Downing Street Declaration. Their personal friendship helped start the Northern Ireland peace process

- No talking to people who used violence and
- No change in the status of Northern Ireland without the clear consent of the majority there.

Reynolds and Major agreed that these principles, rather than the Hume-Adams declaration, should form the basis of a joint statement by the two Prime Ministers.

Once the IRA decided to stop the violence Sinn Féin began to present itself as a 'peace party' implying it was then unionists who were preventing progress

Reynolds sent John Hume's proposed declaration to Major. Major disliked the idea of the British 'persuading' unionists to accept a united Ireland and Reynolds was willing to drop that because he wanted the UUP to find any declaration acceptable. With that gone Major accepted the other points.

THE SHANKILL BOMB AND THE GREYSTEEL MASSACRE

These secret manoeuvres were nearly upset by a new spasm of violence in the North. On 23 October 1993 the IRA set out to bomb UDA leaders it believed were meeting in a room above a betting shop on the Shankill Road. But the bomb went off prematurely. It killed the IRA man carrying it and nine Protestant passers-by. The outrage at this slaughter was compounded when Adams carried the coffin of the bomber at his funeral, though as Reynolds pointed out to Major, that was the only way he could retain leadership of his people. On 30 October 1993 the UDA retaliated by machine-gunning a bar in the quiet village of Greysteel near Derry. Six Catholics and one Protestant died.

THE 'SIX PRINCIPLES'

The Shankill bomb and Adams' action made it impossible to build a declaration on the Hume/Adams document. But on 27 October 1993 the Irish government sidelined it by spelling out 'six principles' which must underlie any peace settlement. They included:

15 DECEMBER 1993: THE DOWNING STREET DECLARATION

On the 15 December the Taoiseach and the Prime Minister met in Downing Street and issued the **Downing Street Declaration**. A short document with just eleven paragraphs, its key sentence read:

'That it is for the people of the island of Ireland alone, between the two parts respectively, to exercise their right of self-determination on the

*basis of consent, freely given, North and South,
to bring about a united Ireland, if that is their
wish.'*

This very complex but carefully crafted sentence
provided both the nationalist and unionist
communities in Ireland with what they wanted:

- For nationalists there was the guarantee that it
  was up to *'the people of the island of Ireland
  alone'* to decide their future.
- For unionists there was the guarantee that
  unity could only come *'on the basis of consent,
  freely given, North and South'*.

This could be the basis for the 'agreed Ireland' that
Hume had proposed.

THE REPUBLICAN RESPONSE

The Downing Street Declaration sparked a debate
within Sinn Féin and the IRA.

- Hard-liners saw little new in it and wanted to
  ignore it.
- Others, including Adams and Martin
  McGuinness wanted to use it as a basis for talks.
  But that could only come after a ceasefire.

In the South Reynolds tempted the republicans
with concessions. He ended the ban on republicans
appearing on radio or TV and set up a Forum for
Peace and Reconciliation to discuss the way
forward. More important was President Clinton's
agreement, in the face of British opposition, to let
Adams attend a conference on Northern Ireland in
New York. But both made clear that these
concessions would only continue if there was a
permanent IRA ceasefire and the decommissioning
of IRA arms.

THE IRA CEASEFIRE OPENS THE WAY FOR PEACE

The republican leadership produced a discussion
document for their members they called TUAS.
They told their members the letters stood for:
'tactical use of armed struggle' but assured the
governments and the Americans that they meant

'totally un-armed strategy'. They also made a last
show of strength by firing mortar bombs at
Heathrow airport, though the bombs were primed
not to go off. This produced an angry reaction
from Reynolds and the Americans as did a limited
ceasefire in March 1994. Finally on 31 August the
IRA announced an unconditional ceasefire.

This was the essential first step that would lead,
after many painful years of negotiation, to the
1998 **Good Friday Agreement** and finally to the
establishment in 2007 of the most unlikely of all
power-sharing Executives with Ian Paisley as Chief
Minister and Martin McGuinness as his Deputy.

QUESTIONS

1 In what way did Sinn Féin policy
   change in 1986? How do you explain
   the change? Did Sinn Féin achieve
   what it hoped for? Why?

2 Why and in what ways did the IRA
   campaign change in the mid-80s?
   Describe two ways in which the British
   responded to it.

3 Outline the nature of the loyalist
   response.

4 Discuss some of the contradictions in
   the IRA/Sinn Féin policies.

5 Read Peter Brooke's speech and say
   why it was important.

6 What were the Hume-Adams talks and
   what were the issues they discussed?

7 Explain the part played by (a) Bill
   Clinton, (b) Albert Reynolds and
   (c) John Major in the peace process.

8 Who signed the Downing Street
   Declaration in 1993 and why was it
   important?

9 Outline the events which led from the
   Downing Street Declaration to the IRA
   ceasefire of 1994.

Exam-Type Questions

LEAVING CERTIFICATE QUESTIONS

Ordinary Level Questions

1 A Part of a speech by Gerry Fitt to the Stormont parliament in 1965

In recent times the Prime Minister [met] ... the Prime Minister of the Republic, Mr. Lemass. That was one of the greatest decisions taken since the inception of the Northern Ireland Parliament and ... was applauded by all sections of reasonable thought in Northern Ireland. It was commonly conceded that at last the Prime Minister had shown himself to be a statesman and Prime Minister of all the people in Northern Ireland.

This decision on the university has completely wrecked anything which was gained from the cross Border meetings. We have a complete division again, but the division this time is not a division on sectarian or religious lines but among the Prime Minister's own people. His own greatest supporters, the people of [Londonderry], have rejected out of hand the reasons which the Government have given for denying the city its just right to this university. (*Parliamentary reports* Vol. 59, page 1553)

1 Name the Prime Minister of Northern Ireland that Fitt is talking about.

2 What action of his did Fitt believe was 'applauded by all sections of reasonable thought in Northern Ireland'?

3 What decision does he think has 'completely wrecked anything that was gained from the cross border meetings'?

4 Who does Fitt think have rejected the reasons given for that decision?

5 What reasons did the Northern Ireland government give for its decision on the location of the new university?

B Write a short paragraph on **one** of the following:

   1 The impact of educational reform in Northern Ireland.

   2 Bernadette Devlin.

   3 Sectarianism in Northern Ireland.

   4 The Civil Rights Movement in Northern Ireland.

C Answer **one** of the following:

   1 How important are the Apprentice Boys of Derry to the cultural identity of unionists in Northern Ireland?

   2 What part did Terence O'Neill play in the history of Northern Ireland?

   3 What led to the Sunningdale Agreement of 1973 and what were its main terms?

   4 Why did Margaret Thatcher agree to make the Anglo-Irish Agreement in 1985?

2 A

1 Who is the speaker and what position did he hold in 1971?

2 Who were 'the minority' he was talking about?

3 What did they hope for in 1971 and did the cartoonist think they would get it?

4 What policy did this man introduce soon after?

5 Give two reasons why the way that policy was implemented annoyed the minority.

B Write a short paragraph on **one** of the following:

1 Gerrymandering in Northern Ireland elections.

2 Bloody Sunday in Derry in January 1972.

3 How Seamus Heaney and other poets responded to the 'Troubles'.

4 How the 'Troubles' affected the Northern Ireland economy.

C Answer **one** of the following:

1 What changes did the Welfare state bring to Northern Ireland society in the 1950s and how did they affect the position of the minority community?

2 How did the controversy over the location of a second university show up the divisions within Northern Ireland?

3 Why did the Sunningdale Agreement fail?

4 How did John Hume as leader of the SDLP seek a political settlement up to 1993?

3 A A Death in Derry

[Father Edward Daly, a Derry priest was watching the banned march on 30 January 1972 when soldiers began to advance towards them. He ran away from them]

… I noticed a young boy running beside me… He caught my attention because he was smiling or laughing…. He seemed about 16 or 17. I did not see anything in his hands. I didn't know his name then, but I later learned that his name was Jackie Duddy…. When we reached the centre of the courtyard, I heard a shot and simultaneously this young boy, just beside me, gasped or groaned loudly. This was the first shot that I had heard since the two or three shots I had heard some time earlier in the afternoon. I glanced around and the young boy just fell on his face. He fell in the middle of the courtyard… [After going back with others to help the boy who was badly wounded] … we decided to make a dash for it. We got up first of all from our knees and I waved the handkerchief, which, by now, was heavily bloodstained. I went in front and the men behind me carried Jackie Duddy… a woman called Mrs McCloskey …. phoned for an ambulance. Then a patrol of soldiers appeared in Waterloo Street and told us to clear off and I asked the people to calm down and kneel down and offer a prayer. The soldiers moved away. I remember one of the women screaming down the street after them shouting, 'He's only a child and you've killed him.' We waited until the ambulance arrived. I am not sure how long it took. It wasn't very long. Jackie Duddy's body was brought to the hospital.

…Then I made my way … to … the Rossville Flats in front of the shops. I was thunderstruck by the scene that met my eyes. Until then, I had no conception of the scale of the horror. I quickly realised that I had witnessed merely a small part of the overall picture. There were dead and dying and wounded everywhere. I administered the last rites to many of them… (from Edward Daly: Mister, Are You a Priest? 2000, pp 189–195)

1 How old was the boy running beside Father Daly and what was his name?

2 What happened to the boy?

3 How did Father Daly and others try to help him?

4 What did Father Daly see when he got to the Rossville Flats?

5 What were the long term results of these events in Derry?

B Write a short paragraph on **one** of the following:

1 The IRA border campaign in the 1950s.

2 Patricia and Conn McCluskey and the Campaign for Social Justice.

3 The IRA hunger strikes.

4 Ian Paisley and the Anglo-Irish Agreement of 1985.

C Answer **one** of the following:

1 How did the ecumenical movement affect Northern Ireland?

2 How did Gerry Adams change IRA tactics after 1979?

3 How did the northern Troubles change southern attitudes towards Northern Ireland?

4 What was the significance of the Downing Street Declaration of 1993?

Higher Level Questions

1 What was the significance of the Apprentice Boys of Derry and the other Loyal Orders in the cultural identity of Northern Irish Protestants?

2 What economic, social and political problems did Lord Brookeborough's government face in Northern Ireland and to what extent had these been solved by the time he retired in 1963?

3 What was the situation of the minority community in Northern Ireland in 1960 and how and why had that changed by 1974?

4 Why did Terence O'Neill's career end in failure?

5 How does the career of Brian Faulkner between 1949 and 1974 reflect political developments within Northern Ireland?

6 What was the background to the 1973 Sunningdale Agreement and why did it end in failure?

7 How did Margaret Thatcher's policy towards Northern Ireland develop between 1979 and 1990?

8 How did the Troubles in Northern Ireland affect the Republic and did they alter southern attitudes towards partition?

9 How did one or more of the following contribute to developments in Northern Ireland: Conn and Patricia McCluskey; Bernadette Devlin, John Hume, Gerry Adams?

10 What developments led to the Downing Street Declaration of 1993 and what was its political significance?

THE PRIME MINISTERS, MINISTERS AND TAOISIGH INVOLVED IN NORTHERN IRELAND FROM 1945–1994

	Prime Minister of Northern Ireland / Secretary of State for Northern Ireland	Prime Minister of the United Kingdom	Taoiseach of the Republic
1945–50	Sir Basil Brooke (Lord Brookeborough) (1943–1963)	Clement Atlee (Labour) (1945–1951)	Éamon de Valera (Fianna Fáil) (1932–1948) John A Costello (Coalition) (1948–1951)
1950–55		Winston Churchill (Conservative) (1951–1955)	Éamon de Valera (1951–1954) John A. Costello (1954–1957)
1955–60		Anthony Eden (Conservative) (1955–1957) Harold Macmillan (Conservative) (1957–1963)	Éamon de Valera (1957–1959)
1960–65	Terence O'Neill (1963–1969)	Alec Douglas Home (Conservative) (1963–1964)	Seán Lemass (Fianna Fáil) (1958–1965)
1965–70	James Chichester Clarke (1969–March 1971)	Harold Wilson (Labour) (1964–1970) Home Secretary: James Callaghan	Jack Lynch (Fianna Fáil) (1965–1973)
1970–75	Brian Faulkner (March 1971–March 1972) William Whitelaw (March 1972–November 1973) Francis Pym (November 1973–February 1974) Brian Faulkner/Gerry Fitt (Sunningdale) (January 1974–May 1974)	Edward Heath (Conservative) (1970–1974) Home Secretary: Reginald Maudling	Liam Cosgrave (Coalition) (1973–1977)
1975–80	Merlyn Rees 1974–1976 Roy Mason 1976–1979	Harold Wilson (Labour) (1974–1976) James Callaghan (Labour) (1976–1979)	Jack Lynch (1977–1979) Charles Haughey (Fianna Fáil) (1979–1981)
1980–85	Humphrey Atkins 1979–1981 James Prior 1981–1984	Margaret Thatcher (Conservative) (1979–1990)	Garret FitzGerald (Coalition) (1981–1982) Charles Haughey (Fianna Fáil)(1982) Garret FitzGerald (Coalition) (1982–1987)
1985–90	Douglas Hurd 1984–1985 Tom King 1985–1989		Charles Haughey (Fianna Fáil) (1987–1992)
1990–95	Peter Brooke 1989–1992 Patrick Mayhew 1992–1997	John Major (Conservative) (1990–1997)	Albert Reynolds (Fianna Fáil) (1992–1994) John Bruton (Coalition) (1994–1997)

Prime Ministers of Northern Ireland are in bold text.

Abstention: Republicans refusing to enter the Dáil, the Northern Ireland parliament or the Commons at Westminster because to do so involved them taking an oath to the king/queen.

Anglo-Irish: The connection between Britain and Ireland.

Bigot: A person with strong views on religion or politics who refuses to accept other people's views as valid or honestly held.

Bigotry: The belief that only one's own views are entitled to respect and acceptance.

Bi-partisan: drawn from two sides of a dispute. In the Northern Irish conflict, the British Conservative and Labour parties followed a 'bi-partisan policy' – that is they agreed on what needed to be done so that when the government changed the policy did not. This bi-partisanship kept the northern conflict from spilling over into Britain and made it easier to find a solution that all British people could accept.

Cabinet: A committee made up of the chief minister and other important ministers, each in charge of a particular area of government (e.g. justice, finance, etc). The Cabinet usually forms the "government" of a country, taking the important decisions about how a country is run (e.g. deciding on taxes or spending priorities or relations with foreign countries.)

Civil rights: The rights people are entitled to as citizens of a democratic society. They usually include: the right to vote, to free speech and a free press, to practice religion, to assemble peacefully, to get a fair trial and not to be tortured.

Civil servants: Officials who carry out the laws passed by parliament or the policies decided by ministers.

Constituency: The district or area whose people elect one or more members of parliament or of local councils. In local government, constituencies were often called 'wards'.

Cultural / Ethnic identity: a sense of the people one belongs to – e.g. Catholics in Northern Ireland saw themselves as 'Irish' while many Protestants saw themselves as 'British'.

Cultural traditions: The religion, history, music, poetry, games, marches, festivals etc from which people draw their sense of who they are (i.e. their cultural/ethnic identity).

Discrimination: Unfair treatment of a person or group of people because of their religion, age, gender, etc.

Ecumenism: A movement aimed at ending the divisions among Christians. It began among the various Protestant Churches and was strengthened by their common sufferings under Fascist and Communist regimes from the 1920s. The Catholic Church began to support ecumenism after John XXIII became Pope in 1958.

Extradition: Sending people accused of committing a crime back to be tried in the country where the crime was committed.

Gerrymandering: Drawing the boundaries of a constituency in such a way that one party is more likely to win than another.

Government of Northern Ireland: Through the period covered by this book several forms of government existed in Northern Ireland:

- **Majority rule:** the system that existed up to 1972 in which the Unionist Party had a majority in the Stormont parliament and ruled alone.

- **Direct rule from London:** The system that existed after Stormont was abolished in 1972. A Secretary of State (Minister) was appointed by the British government to rule Northern Ireland directly. Northern Ireland politicians had little influence on his policies.

- **Power-sharing:** A Northern Ireland based government but one which contained representatives elected by both nationalist and unionist communities. The Sunningdale Executive was a power-sharing government and so is the one established under the 1998 Good Friday Agreement.

Internment: Imprisoning people without trying them in a court and producing evidence of their guilt.

Intolerance: Being unwilling to accept and respect the views of others; rejecting the validity of points of view other than one's own; being unwilling to allow others to follow their own customs and beliefs.

Kingdom: A state in which the

head of state is a hereditary king or queen. Up to 1921 all of Ireland belonged to the United Kingdom of Great Britain and Ireland. After partition, only Northern Ireland remained part of the United Kingdom.

Loyalists: People who were loyal to the king/queen who was the head of the United Kingdom (as opposed to the nationalists who were 'disloyal'). At first 'loyalist' and 'unionist' meant the same thing but as the conflict in Northern Ireland continued, the word 'loyalist' was used only for unionists who supported violence, while 'unionist' was kept for those who wanted to use peaceful, constitutional means to achieve their aims.

Ministry/Department: The Minister and civil servants who deal with one aspect of a country's government or put the Cabinet's decisions into operation. The Northern government usually used 'Ministry' while in the South, 'Department' was preferred.

Nationalist: In Irish history a nationalist was a person who wanted Ireland to have its own government so that Irish people could make the important decisions about the country. Most, though not all, Irish nationalists were Catholics. After partition, nationalists within Northern Ireland were those people who wanted to re-unite with the South. As the northern conflict developed the word 'nationalist' was usually used for those who only used peaceful, constitutional means.

Opposition party: In a democratic country, the main political party which opposes the policies of the current government. It hopes to persuade the voters to support it and to form the government after the next election. In other words it provides voters with **an alternative government** and gives them a choice of leaders and policies. Because of the way Northern Ireland was set up, it was impossible for this kind of Opposition Party to emerge.

Papist/pape: A mildly insulting way of referring to Roman Catholics. It comes from the fact that the Pope is the head of their church.

Paramilitary: A private organisation with some of the characteristics of an army – e.g. guns, uniforms, drills and parades. No democratic government can allow paramilitary organisations to develop in its territory.

Partition: To divide into two or more parts. In Ireland the word is usually used as a short way of referring to the division of the country in 1920 into two areas, one dominated by nationalists, one by unionists.

Political party: A group of people with shared ideas who try to get elected to parliament so that they can influence the way in which their country is run.

Power-sharing: A situation in which both unionists and nationalists could share in the government of Northern Ireland. The first example of power-sharing came in 1974 after the Sunningdale Agreement when Brian Faulkner (a Protestant unionist) and Gerry Fitt (a Catholic nationalist) jointly led the Executive which was to rule Northern Ireland.

Propaganda: Presenting news/information in such a way as to make one's own side look good and the other side look bad.

In the Northern conflict all sides used propaganda extensively and it has sometimes been describes as a 'propaganda war'.

Republic/republicans: A republic is a state in which the head of state is an elected President. In Irish history the word 'republic' usually meant an Irish state that included the whole island of Ireland and was completely separate from Britain. People who supported this aim were called 'republicans'. As the Northern conflict developed the word 'republican' was usually used for nationalists who supported the aims and tactics of the IRA (the use of force).

Sectarianism: Judging people by the religion (sect) or ethnic or political group to which they belong; intolerance of others who belong to a different religion (sect) or ethnic group or with a different point of view from one's own; refusing to treat people with different religious or political or ethnic identity fairly – e.g. in jobs or voting.

Sovereign government: A government totally independent of any other. The British and Irish governments were sovereign; the Northern government was not.

'Stormont': A short-hand way of referring to the government/ parliament of Northern Ireland. It comes from Stormont Castle where they were housed. In the same way, 'Westminster' is used for the British government in London.

Terrorism: The use of violence or the threat of violence against the public in order to achieve political or ideological aims. In Northern Ireland republicans used terror to force the British to leave and loyalists used terror to intimidate

Catholics and stop them supporting a united Ireland.

The labour movement: All the organisations like the trade unions which try to improve the living standards of workers. They are represented in parliament by the Labour Party.

Tolerance: A willingness to accept and respect the views of others as valid; being open to the ideas of others; being willing to allow others freedom to follow their customs and beliefs.

Unionists: People who wanted Northern Ireland to remain part of the United Kingdom of Great Britain and Northern Ireland. They saw themselves as 'loyal' to Britain, unlike the 'disloyal' nationalists, so originally they also called themselves 'loyalists'. But as the conflict developed in Northern Ireland, the word 'unionist' came to mean only those unionists who rejected violence and used peaceful, lawful methods.

Voting methods: Two methods of voting have been used in Ireland since 1920:

- **Proportional Representation (PR):** People vote for candidates in order of their choice and seats are distributed among parties in proportion to the votes cast for them.
- **'First past the post':** the candidate with most votes wins. This is fair when there are only two candidates but is unfair if there are more than two as the winning candidate may get well under half of the votes cast.

Working Class: People working in factories or in poorly paid, unskilled jobs or living on unemployment pay.

MAP OF KEY LOCATIONS IN NORTHERN IRELAND

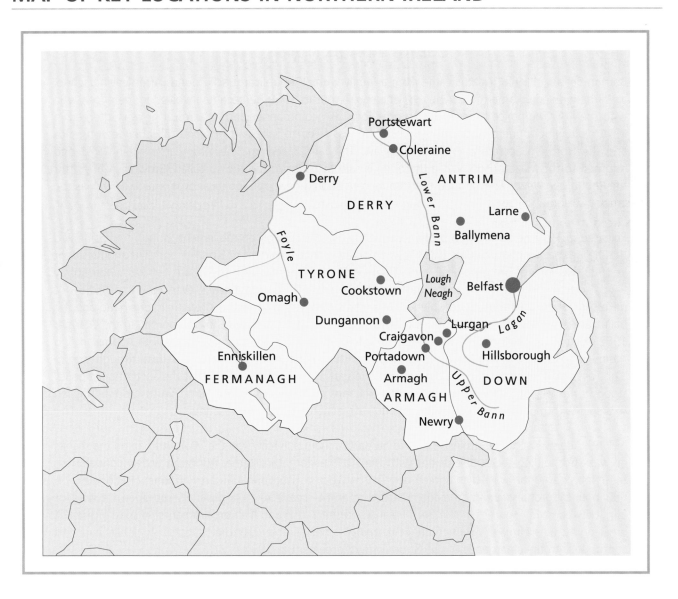

GERRY ADAMS (1948–   )

Born in Belfast in 1948, Adams came from a family with a Republican background. After leaving school at 17 he worked as a barman. When violence broke out in 1969 he became involved in 'defence work' with the IRA. The police believed he was the local IRA commander and as a result he was interned in 1971. Following a brief IRA ceasefire in 1972 he was freed to take part in secret talks between the IRA and the Northern Secretary, William Whitelaw. The talks failed and he was rearrested in 1973 and returned to the Maze prison. While there, he is said to have written the so-called 'Brownie Articles' for the *Republican News*. They argued that republicans should develop a political programme as well as the 'armed struggle'.

Released in 1977 he remained a prominent member of the republican movement though he has denied that he was a senior figure in the IRA. He was elected as Vice-President of Sinn Féin in 1978 and President in 1983. His idea of more political involvement gained support during the hunger strikes when Bobby Sands' election showed that many nationalists would vote for republicans even when they did not necessarily share their attitude to violence. This new strategy, known as the 'Armalite in one hand and the ballot box in the other', led to Sinn Féin contesting elections on both sides of the border. In the October 1982 election to the Northern Ireland Assembly, five Sinn Féin candidates won seats, with Adams among them. He followed this in 1983 by winning Gerry Fitt's Westminster seat in West Belfast, though true to Sinn Féin's abstentionist policy he did not take the seat. However he believed that the abstentionist policy stood in the way of Sinn Féin success in Dáil elections and in 1986 he got Sinn Féin to drop it. This led to a split with more traditional republicans but the majority stayed with Adams.

In 1992 Adams lost his Westminster seat to his party's main political rival, the SDLP. But behind the scenes he was also holding secret discussions with the SDLP leader, John Hume. Although widely condemned, these talks paved the way to an agreed position between constitutional and revolutionary nationalists on how political progress could be made. That led to an IRA ceasefire in August 1994 to open the way for talks between all the parties in Northern Ireland and the British and Irish governments. In spite of the IRA breaking its ceasefire in 1996, Sinn Féin gained considerable electoral success in 1997 and this contributed to the emergence of the Good Friday Agreement in 1997.

BERNADETTE DEVLIN (1947–   )

Bernadette Devlin (McAliskey) was born in Cookstown, County Tyrone in 1947. While a student in Queen's University Belfast, she became involved with the civil rights movement and was involved in all of the main marches organised by the Northern Ireland Civil Rights Association (NIRCA) in 1968 and 1969. Late in 1968 she became involved in the radical leftwing student group, the **People's Democracy (PD)** and stood against Chichester Clarke in the 1969 Stormont general election.

An articulate speaker, she often appeared on TV. This gave her a high profile and led to her selection as a 'Unity' candidate to stand against a unionist in the Westminster by-election for Mid-Ulster in March 1969. She won the seat, and at 21 became the youngest woman ever elected to the House of Commons. She kept the seat in the general election of 1970.

She took part in the 'Battle of the Bogside' in Derry in August 1969 and in 1970 received a six months jail sentence for her activities. After Bloody Sunday in January 1972 she punched the British Home Secretary Reginald Maudling after he said in the Commons that the British army fired in self-defence.

After losing her Westminster seat in February 1974, Devlin still supported left-wing causes and helped to found the **Irish Republican Socialist Party** (IRSP) when it broke away from the Official IRA. But she broke with it when it was involved in violence. She attacked the 'Peace People' and in 1979 stood for election to the European Parliament to publicise the republican prisoners who were engaged in the blanket protests against the British government's policy of criminalisation. Although republicans opposed her decision, she won over 38,000 votes. This result showed republicans that there were many nationalists who would vote for them and this helped move Sinn Féin towards politics.

Devlin continued to play a prominent part in the campaign for the hunger strikers. During it loyalist paramilitaries attacked Devlin and her husband Michael McAliskey in February 1981, leaving them seriously wounded. After she recovered she continued to campaign on left wing issues and has been critical of Sinn Féin's part in the peace process.

BRIAN FAULKNER (1921–1977)

Brian Faulkner was born in County Down in 1921. His study of law at Queens was interrupted by World War II, during which he worked at his family's shirt-making firm. Elected to Stormont as a Unionist MP for East Down in 1949, he became Minister of Home Affairs in 1959 during the IRA's border campaign. His tough approach to it earned him the support of right-wing unionists. He hoped to succeed Brookeborough as Prime Minister in 1963 but leading Unionists chose Terence O'Neill instead.

O'Neill made him Minister of Commerce. He energetically pursued industrial development and was successful in persuading foreign companies to set up in Northern Ireland. But his relationship with O'Neill was always tense and he was concerned at the way O'Neill handled the civil rights campaign. He resigned in January 1969 in protest at the package of reforms O'Neill introduced on the orders of the British government. This was the last blow to O'Neill who resigned in April when he did not get a good enough result in the general election. In the vote for a new leader, Faulkner lost by one vote to James Chichester Clarke.

Faulkner agreed to serve in Chichester Clarke's government as Minister of Development and worked hard to push through the reforms he had previously opposed. After conditions deteriorated, Chichester Clarke resigned in March 1971. William Craig stood against Faulkner for the leadership of the UUP but was defeated by a wide margin.

Faulkner began by reaching out to non-unionists. He gave a Cabinet post to a Labour MP and proposed powerful committees in Stormont which could be chaired by nationalists. But this good beginning was destroyed when he introduced internment on 9 August. This increased nationalist alienation and strengthened the IRA. Violence grew over the rest of the year, culminating in Bloody Sunday in Derry in January 1972. In March, the Prime Minister, Edward Heath, told him the British were taking responsibility for security and the Unionist government resigned in protest. That ended the Stormont regime and began the period of 'direct rule' from London. William Whitelaw was appointed the first Secretary of State for Northern Ireland.

At first Faulkner joined with Craig and Vanguard to oppose direct rule but later recognised that power-sharing was the only way forward. He took part in talks with the SDLP and the British and Irish governments late in 1973 and he signed the Sunningdale Agreement. He was to head a 'power-sharing Executive' in coalition with the SDLP but many unionists were alienated by the plan for a Council of Ireland which seemed to point towards a united Ireland. In December 1973 Faulkner lost a vote in the Ulster Unionist Council. He resigned from the Unionist Party and set up the Unionist Party of Northern Ireland.

In January 1974 he took his place as head of the new Executive. It was soon in trouble after Heath called a general election and unionists opposed to the Executive won 11 out of the 12 Westminster seats. In May the Ulster Workers' Council called a strike against the Executive. Many unionists supported the strikers and the British army did not intervene. After two weeks Faulkner resigned and the power-sharing experiment came to an end.

Faulkner's party did badly in the elections that followed. His influence was drastically reduced and he retired from politics in 1977, getting a seat in the House of Lords as Lord Faulkner of Downpatrick. He died shortly afterwards in a hunting accident.

SEAMUS HEANEY (1939–)

Seamus Heaney was born on a small farm called Mossbawn in Co Derry in 1939, the eldest of nine children. His early experiences on the farm helped to shape his poetry and Mossbawn and its surroundings are the 'country of the mind' from which he first drew his inspiration.

At 12 Heaney won a scholarship to St. Columb's College, a Catholic boarding school in Derry. This move, which he describes as from 'the earth of farm labour to the heaven of education' has been a recurrent theme in his work. While in school, his four-year-old brother Christopher was killed in an accident, an event that inspired two poems, *Mid-Term Break* and *The Blackbird of Glanmore*.

Heaney went on to study Latin, Irish and English in Queen's University in Belfast and then to teach in the city. He first attracted public attention with the poems he published in *Death of a Naturalist* in 1966. Commentators grouped him with several other young writers like Michael Longley and Derek Mahon as forming part of a "Northern School" of Irish writing. He became a lecturer in Queen's in 1966.

The outbreak of the troubles in 1969 forced him to consider the responsibility of the poet in times of conflict. Should a poet pursue creative freedom or express his obligations as a citizen? These concerns are teased out in numerous articles and prose essays collected in *The Government of the Tongue* (1988) and other books. Mostly he chose not to confront the conflict directly but it echoes through many of his poems. He continued to identify with the Gaelic past as is evident in his translations from the Irish like his version of the old Irish story of *Suibhne Gealt* in *Sweeney Astray* (1982).

In 1972 Heaney and his family left Belfast and settled in Co Wicklow, where he worked as a poet and freelance writer. Later he had a teaching post in Dublin and after he resigned from that had an arrangement with Harvard University which allowed him to divide his time between Ireland and the United States. In 1980 he became involved in the Field Day Theatre Company, based in Derry. In association with the poets Seamus Deane and Tom Paulin, the playwright, Brian Friel and the actor Stephen Rea, Field Day sought to explore the crisis in Northern Ireland through plays, poems and pamphlets. In 1990 the company produced *The Cure at Troy*, Heaney's translation of one of Sophocles's plays. He has received many honours, the most important of which was the Nobel Prize in Literature in 1995.

JOHN HUME (1937–   )

Born in Derry in 1937, John Hume got his secondary education in St Columb's College in Derry and received his BA degree in Maynooth. He returned to teach in St Columb's and got involved in a number of social activities such as the Credit Union. In 1964-5 he was actively involved in the campaign to get Northern Ireland's second university for Derry, and chaired the University for Derry Committee set up in January 1965. But Terence O'Neill's government decided to accept the advice of the Lockwood Committee and locate it in Coleraine instead of Derry. This convinced Hume that O'Neill's promise of reform was not serious and that only direct action would achieve results.

Hume then became involved in the Civil Rights campaign. After the violence which followed a civil rights march on 5 October 1968, he was elected to the Derry Citizens' Action Committee and tried to ensure that later protests were peaceful. In the 1969 Stormont election he became MP for the Foyle. In 1970 he worked with other anti-unionist MPs to create a new party, the Social Democratic and Labour Party (SDLP). As one of its leading members he was involved in the negotiations leading to the Sunningdale Agreement in December 1975 which set up a power-sharing executive to administer Northern Ireland and a Council of Ireland to provide an 'Irish dimension' for nationalists. When the Executive was set up in January 1974 he became Minister of Commerce, dealing with the economic problems caused by the Loyalist workers' strike.

The failure of the Sunningdale Agreement and of the Constitutional Convention that followed convinced Hume that a new approach was needed. He believed that an internal, Northern Ireland solution was not enough. To be successful any agreement must include politicians from the United States and Europe as well as from Northern Ireland, the republic and Britain. Other leading members of the SDLP disagreed with him on this. In November 1979 Gerry Fitt resigned and Hume was elected leader. Earlier that year he had been elected to the European parliament and in 1983 he was elected to Westminster. These positions gave him the status and the contacts from which to interest foreign leaders in his proposals.

He refused to lead the SDLP into Humphrey Atkins' Constitutional Conference in 1980 or in James Prior's plan for 'rolling devolution' in 1982 because they focused merely on an internal settlement. He did however take part in Garret FitzGerald's New Ireland Forum in Dublin in 1983–4 at which constitutional nationalists tried to produce a new framework through which Irish unity could be achieved.

The 1985 Anglo-Irish Agreement was the first sign that his ideas might be influencing developments. But this could produce no immediate results while the IRA continued its murderous campaign. To encourage it to consider other options Hume began secret negotiations with Gerry Adams, President of Sinn Féin, and other republicans in 1988. Although widely criticised, the talks laid the basis for the future 'peace process', leading to the IRA ceasefire in 1994. Hume led his party into the talks which finally produced the Good Friday Agreement in April 1998. In 1998 his role in bringing peace was recognised when he and David Trimble were jointly awarded the Nobel Peace Prize.

JAMES MOLYNEAUX (1920–   )

Born into a farming family in Co Antrim, James Molyneaux served in the RAF in World War II. After it he became a farmer and was also actively involved in the Ulster Unionist Party and in the loyal orders. In 1970 he was elected to the Westminster parliament as UUP MP for South Antrim. He opposed the Sunningdale Agreement and the power-sharing Executive. When Brian Faulkner lost the support of the Ulster Unionist Council in January 1974 and resigned, Molyneaux stood for the leadership but was beaten by Harry West. Later that year he became the leader of the Ulster Unionist MPs at Westminster. He took advantage of the weakness of Jim Callaghan's Labour Government in the late 1970s to negotiate a number of concessions to Unionists including increasing the number of Northern Ireland seats at Westminster from 12 to 17.

He succeeded West as party leader in 1979. The party had been weakened by bad organisation and West's weak leadership and its position was threatened by the growing popularity of Ian Paisley's DUP. Molyneaux's attempts to revitalise it were hampered by divisions among Unionists about future policy. Should they work for Northern Ireland to be integrated into the British system or should they press for a return to devolved government? Molyneaux's preference for integration led to criticism from some more of his followers.

Feeling that more could be won by negotiation than by confrontation, he took his seat in the Northern Ireland Assembly elected in 1982 as part of the plan for 'rolling devolution' devised by the Secretary of State for Northern Ireland, James Prior. The plan collapsed and Molyneaux opposed the British attempt to improve relations with the republic but refused to take part in talks. The 1985 Anglo-Irish Agreement took him by surprise. He joined with Ian Paisley in opposing it. As part of the protest he resigned his seat in Westminster but won it back in the subsequent by-election. He drew back from the protests when the DUP seemed to be working with loyalist paramilitaries.

In the early 1990s he led the UUP delegation to the all-party talks with the main political parties in Northern Ireland, (apart from Sinn Féin) and the London and Dublin governments. When these ended in failure Molyneaux continued to call for their resumption but this failed. The British and Irish governments pursued an alternative strategy which led to the Downing Street Declaration of 15 December 1993. Though sceptical, Molyneaux gave it a guarded welcome. Discontent with his leadership began to emerge and in 1995 he resigned. He remained active in politics, opposing the Good Friday Agreement and opposing power-sharing. He was appointed to the Lords as Lord Molyneaux of Killead in 1997.

PATRICIA McCLUSKEY, CONN McCLUSKEY

Patricia McShane worked as a social worker in Glasgow before returning home to marry Conn McCluskey, a medical doctor living in Dungannon, Co Tyrone. The local unionist council was unwilling to give houses to local Catholics, even when they were living in very bad slum conditions. Disturbed by how bad housing affected women and especially children, Patricia helped to found the Homeless Citizens League in 1963.

Unlike previous Catholic groups, their aim was not Irish unity but civil rights. They argued that if they were to be forced to live in the United Kingdom they were entitled to the same rights as other citizens elsewhere in the United Kingdom. To support their case they began systematically to collect evidence of discrimination in jobs and housing in the gerrymandered councils in the west of Northern Ireland.

To put pressure on other councils and the Unionist government to improve housing, end discrimination and improve conditions for Catholics, the McCluskeys were among the founders of the **Campaign for Social Justice** (CSJ) in 1964. They collected data about gerrymandering and discrimination in employment, housing, and public appointments in Northern Ireland. In 1964 they published their findings in a pamphlet called: *Northern Ireland, The plain truth.*

In 1964 Patricia McCluskey and three other CSJ members were elected to Dungannon Council. She presented her data to prominent politicians in Westminster where a Campaign for Democracy in Ulster (CDU) was set up but the British and Northern Ireland governments took no effective action at this time. Patricia McCluskey became a member of the Northern Ireland Civil Rights Association (NICRA) when it was founded in 1967.

TERENCE O'NEILL (1914–1990)

Terence O'Neill belonged to an aristocratic family with large estates in County Antrim. He was educated in England and served with the Irish Guards in World War II. He went to live in Northern Ireland after the war and in 1946 was elected to Stormont as the Unionist MP for the Bannside constituency. After holding a number of junior positions, he became Minister for Home Affairs in 1955. In 1956 he was promoted to Minister for Finance. When Lord Brookeborough retired in 1963, O'Neill became Prime Minister.

O'Neill wanted to modernise Northern Ireland while retaining the supremacy of the Unionist Party. His economic policy involved the central government becoming more involved in economic planning and development. He set up committees to suggest reforms in education, transport and town planning. He also encouraged multinational companies to set up there to replace the jobs being lost in the traditional industries of linen and shipbuilding.

Part of his modernising plan involved improving relationships with the Irish republic and with the Catholic minority within Northern Ireland. He invited the Taoiseach, Seán Lemass to visit Belfast in 1965 and visited Dublin himself shortly afterwards. These visits laid plans for cross-border co-operation in economic areas like tourism and transport. He also made some small conciliatory gestures towards the minority.

Many unionists were alarmed by these actions and their concerns were expressed by Ian Paisley who mounted an 'O'Neill must go' campaign. At the same time Catholics noted that he made no significant concessions. He failed to appoint Catholics to various committees. He accepted the Lockwood Report that Northern Ireland's second university should be in Protestant Coleraine rather than in mainly Catholic Derry. They concluded that only direct action could lead to reform and many of them supported the civil rights campaign which began in 1967. As violence flared in Derry, O'Neill tried to strengthen his own position by calling an election for February 1969. The gamble failed and by April 1969 as the situation continued to deteriorate he resigned as Prime Minister. A few months later he also gave up his Stormont seat which was won in the by-election by Ian Paisley. O'Neill moved to England and was given a seat in the Lords as Lord O'Neill of the Maine. He died in 1990.

IAN PAISLEY (1926–   )

Ian Paisley was born in Lurgan, Co. Armagh, the son of a Baptist minister. In 1946 his father ordained him as a minister and in 1951 he founded the Free Presbyterian Chruch of which he was Moderator (head). A fundamentalist Protestant who believed the Bible to be the word of God, he first came to public notice for his attacks on the ecumenical movement which encouraged better relations between Protestants and Roman Catholics.

Paisley also saw Terence O'Neill's gestures towards the Catholic minority in Northern Ireland as a betrayal of the interests of Ulster Protestants. He campaigned against O'Neill, accusing him of weakening the link with Britain through his meetings with the republic's Taoiseach, Seán Lemass in 1965 and launched an 'O'Neill must go' campaign. The emergence of the Civil Rights campaign won him the support of some unionists, especially those who felt their interests had been neglected by O'Neill's government. He formed the Ulster Protestant Volunteers and began to organise counter-demonstrations to coincide with civil rights marches. In November 1968 Paisley was arrested during one of these protests and he was given a jail sentence. Although he always denied any link to loyalist paramilitaries, some of them certainly supported him and claimed to be acting in his name.

Paisley founded the **Protestant Unionist Party** and in February 1969 came close to beating O'Neill in the Stormont general election. This fatally undermined the Prime Minister who resigned soon after. Paisley then won his Stormont seat and shortly afterwards he was elected to the Westminster parliament as the MP for North Antrim. In September 1971 he and other dissident unionists formed the **Democratic Unionist Party (DUP)**. They opposed the reforms that Chichester Clarke and Brian Faulkner introduced in response to pressure from Britain.

After direct rule was imposed in March 1972, the DUP worked for the restoration of Stormont. They took their seats in the Northern Ireland Assembly elected in 1973 but vehemently opposed the idea of power-sharing and a Council of Ireland. Ian Paisley was prominent during the Ulster Workers' Council strike that brought down the power-sharing Executive. He attended the Constitutional Convention (1975–6) and supported its demand for a restoration of devolved government. When that was refused, he led another workers' strike but it was defeated in 1977. In spite of that he topped the poll in the first direct election to the European Parliament in 1979.

Relations between the Ulster Unionist Party and the DUP were bad as they competed for the support of unionist voters. In 1985, however, they co-operated in opposing the Anglo-Irish Agreement. Paisley worked closely with loyalist paramilitaries and this put off many moderate unionists. Paisley loudly condemned every move in the emerging 'peace process' including any talks with the SDLP or the Dublin government. He condemned the Downing Street Declaration of 1993 as a 'sell out' of the Protestant people of Ulster. But from 1996 he got more involved, though he attacked the 1998 Good Friday Agreement and campaigned for a 'No' vote in the referendum that followed. He gradually softened his opposition to power-sharing and in 2007 became head of an Executive with Martin McGuinness of Sinn Féin as his deputy.

MARGARET THATCHER (1925–   )

Margaret Thatcher was born in England in 1925, studied science at Oxford and later became a barrister. In Oxford she joined the Conservative Party and in 1959 was elected an MP. When Edward Heath unexpectedly won the 1970 election, he appointed her as Education Secretary. After the Conservatives lost to Labour in 1974, she challenged Heath and was elected party leader in 1975. She won the 1979 general election, mainly because of Britain's economic decline under the Labour government.

Thatcher was committed to defeating the IRA, which had assassinated her Northern Ireland advisor, Airey Neave shortly before the election. She refused to negotiate with the republican hunger-strikers, ignoring pleas from the Dublin government and many other groups. Although she strongly supported Northern Ireland's place in the United Kingdom, her friend, William Whitelaw, persuaded her that power-sharing between Protestants and Catholics was the best way to protect the Union. She allowed her Northern Ireland Secretaries, Humphrey Atkins and James Prior to try to organise talks between the leaders of the two communities. But she did little to encourage the talks and was not too surprised when they failed.

Her main interest was in security and for this reason she was willing to seek better relations with the Dublin government. She wanted them to seal the border and extradite republican suspects. After a good start in 1979, progress was delayed by the hunger strikes and the 1982 Falklands war in which Charles Haughey opposed Britain.

The re-election of Garret FitzGerald as Taoiseach late in 1982 helped to improve the situation. Thatcher trusted him though their relationship deteriorated briefly in 1984 when she dismissed the recommendations of the New Ireland Forum with the brusque 'OUT' 'OUT' 'OUT'.

Talks resumed soon after leading to the signing of the Anglo-Irish Agreement at Hillsborough, Co Down in November 1985. To the fury of unionists, the Agreement allowed the Irish government to have a say in Northern Ireland affairs and created a permanent Secretariat of civil servants from both governments in Maryfield near Belfast. Thatcher withstood the unionist 'Ulster Says No' campaign but grew disillusioned with the Agreement because it failed to deliver the improvements in security she had hoped for. She resigned as Conservative leader in 1990. She expressed doubts about the 'peace process' and criticised the 1998 Good Friday Agreement for allowing the early release of paramilitary prisoners.

INDEX

Politics and Society
in Northern Ireland
1949–1993

LATER MODERN IRISH HISTORY TOPIC 5

M.E.COLLINS

Edco